This book is filled with practical hel[...]
—Dale O'Shields, [...]
Redeemer, Gaithersburg, MD

Roland is an extraordinary individual who overcame a less than desirable family background to be a dynamic husband and father. His personal life, knowledge of the Scriptures, and leadership at National Fatherhood Initiative have contributed to making *Bad Dads of the Bible* an extraordinary book!
—Matt Bennett, *Founder and President of Christian Union*

A great read. Roland Warren has thirty years working on "Dads." He gives great insight on life with dads and life without dads. You will love the book but be appalled by the problems without dads. Pass the book on. Each of us can be a part of the solutions. Kudos to Roland for this eye-opener.
—Red McCombs, *Owner, McCombs Enterprises;*
Co-Founder, Clear Channel Communications;
Former Owner—San Antonio Spurs,
Denver Nuggets, and Minnesota Vikings

As an eyewitness to the poverty and despair of millions in America and around the world, I can say with conviction that a remarkable proportion of the world's social problems can be traced to a single cause: the dysfunction of men as fathers, husbands, and leaders. Roland Warren has a big idea in this book: help men become better fathers and we can not only change our country, but can also change the world.
—Richard Stearns, *President of World Vision US*
and author of Unfinished

Roland Warren's personal and professional experience gives him a unique perspective on the influence fathers wield in their children's lives—whether for good or for bad. His insight into the lives of dads talked about in Scripture makes this book a must-read for anyone who wants to hand down a dynamic, healthy legacy to their children.

—Jim Liske, *CEO, Prison Fellowship Ministries*

There are few men in our nation who are more tuned in to the present demands of fatherhood. Roland serves every dad with his keen insights from Scripture on how to avoid costly mistakes and instead build a godly legacy through rich relationships with our precious children.

—Brian Doyle, *President, Iron Sharpens Iron*

The greatest regrets men experience come from broken family relationships when God-designed streams of living water become tepid swamps. Roland Warren knows how to help dads get out of the swamp, back to where the good water flows clean and pure. Invite *Bad Dads of the Bible* to help you find the better you!

—Wes Yoder, *Author of Bond of Brothers: Connecting with Other Men beyond Work, Weather and Sports*

BAD DADS

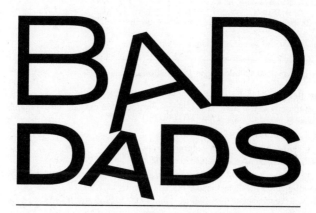

OF THE BIBLE

—
8 MISTAKES
EVERY
GOOD DAD
CAN AVOID
—

ROLAND C. WARREN

 ZONDERVAN®

ZONDERVAN

Bad Dads of the Bible
Copyright © 2013 by Roland C. Warren

This title is also available as a Zondervan ebook. Visit www.zondervan.com/ebooks.

Requests for information should be addressed to:

Zondervan, *Grand Rapids, Michigan* 49530

Library of Congress Cataloging-in-Publication Data

Warren, Roland C.
    Bad dads of the Bible : 8 lessons every good dad can learn from them /
    Roland C. Warren. — 1st [edition].
        pages cm
    Includes bibliographical references and index.
    ISBN 978-0-310-33716-4 (softcover)
        1. Fathers in the Bible. 2. Bible. Old Testament — Criticism, interpretation, etc.
    3. Fatherhood — Religious aspects — Christianity. I. Title.
    BS579.F3W37 2014
    248.8'421 — dc23   2013020618

Cover design: Tim Green/ Faceout Studio
Interior design: Matthew Van Zomeren

Printed in the United States of America

13 14 15 16 17 18 19 20 /DCI/ 20 19 18 17 16 15 14 13 12 11 10 9 8 7 6 5 4 3 2 1

To my dearest wife, Yvette,
who gave me the gift of fatherhood,
and to my sons, Jamin and Justin,
who give me more joy than they will ever know.

To my mother, Angie Cohen.
Thank you for being there.

In loving memory of Jeffrey "Jay" Young
(1961 – 2012).
A good dad.

CONTENTS

FOREWORD

WHEN MY DAD ASKED ME to write this foreword, I initially demurred. "Find someone famous," I told him. "You need to sell books, and given your network, I'm sure you could tap someone with considerable esteem to write on your behalf." He responded with a chuckle, as he usually does, then said, "There's no one better to write about your father than you." So here we are.

For most of my life I was a churchgoer, and as most people who attend services each Sunday, you tend to hear the same stories over and over again. The exploits of Abraham, Isaac, Jacob, and David are not new fodder, and scores of theologians and pastors have pored over the texts to find new ways to explain them. There is nothing new under the sun, as they say. So when my father said that he was going to explore the great men of the Bible in their roles as fathers, I was struck by how original the concept was.

There is a tendency to read history of any kind as a litany of great things men and women have done. As a result, we tend to sugarcoat the indiscretions and ultimate failings of even those we hold in great esteem. My father pulls no such punches with *Bad Dads of the Bible.* What you'll find is a complicated and, at times, troubling picture of the "great" men of the Bible. I believe his intent is not to overshadow what tremendous virtues they might have had, but rather to make them relatable characters whose foibles and shortcomings reflect the nature of man.

Recently, my father floated the idea of "congruence" to me. In geometry, two shapes are congruent if they are the same size and shape. He used that as an analogy to relay the idea that a man's public and private life should match. So often great men leave their home life behind as they pursue fame and fortune. There is certainly meaning in leaving one's mark on the world, but so often, it is at great personal cost to their families and friends. Moreover, the effects are multigenerational, leaving the residue of pain and disappointment on future men and women.

I am so fortunate to have a father who views the act of fathering as a trade, as something to be learned and developed over time. Reading the draft of *Bad Dads of the Bible* was so moving, reminding me of all the little things my father did — asking about my day, playing video games with me, hugging me for no reason — that were part of a larger "daddying" system. Even more fortunate is that now you, the reader, can learn much to enrich your own life and improve your skill as a father.

A good friend of mine recently reached out to her birth father, who, for a variety of reasons, had not been a part of her life. Her expectations were low. She hardly knew this man, after all, and at best, she hoped they could stay in touch as friends. His response to her was wonderful. Her words to him filled him with joy, and he started a lovely correspondence with his newfound daughter. What struck her most was how welcome and ultimately needed those words of affirmation were, so much so, that she wished that she had them her whole life. It was the wonderful beginning of a much-needed reconciliation.

Every father has a choice to make about what kind of dad he will be. In every man there is great potential for good and for harm. My hope is that *Bad Dads of the Bible* will be a lamp in the darkness and a guide for your feet as a father.

—*Jamin Warren*

ACKNOWLEDGMENTS

FIRST AND FOREMOST, I want to thank God, who is the author and the finisher of my faith ... and this book. He graciously blessed me with the idea for this book many years ago. However, writing a book, especially my first one, was a challenging endeavor. I am the type of person who is constantly in motion, and it took a lot to muster the disciplined stillness that writing a book requires. Frankly, I am embarrassed to say that I had a "Moses moment" or two, where I was hopeful that God would find someone else to do what he clearly wanted me to do. But God, like a good Father, sent just the right set of "Aarons" into my life at just the right moments to encourage me, and when needed, to give me a loving but swift kick in the fanny to keep me going. For this I am eternally thankful.

Certainly my pastor, Dale O'Shields of the Church of Redeemer in Gaithersburg, Maryland, was one of these important people. As soon as I told him about the idea for this book, he said enthusiastically, "You have to write it!" Author Don Miller was another such friend. At just the right moment, he sent me a fantastic book called *The War of Art*, which is a compelling "just do it" manual for anyone who seeks to do something creative. In addition, I am truly grateful for the support of Vince DiCaro, who collaborated with me on writing projects while I was with

ACKNOWLEDGMENTS

National Fatherhood Initiative. Despite his daunting work schedule and his responsibilities as husband and father, he spent nights and weekends reading the manuscript to catch typos and split infinitives and to make sure that I was expressing myself in a way that would engage and encourage fathers.

On the Zondervan front, I owe a special thanks to Don Gates, vice president of marketing for trade books, who championed this project within his firm. Also, I want to thank Carolyn McCready, Lori Vanden Bosch, Jim Ruark, and Londa Alderink for their terrific editorial and marketing support to make sure that this book would honor God and inspire its readers.

In addition, I would like to thank my sons, Jamin and Justin, who gave me lots of stories and insights for the book, and who were forgiving when I made a "bad dad" mistake or two on my fathering journey. Being their father is a joy and pleasure, and I am thankful to God for the opportunity to be in their lives and have them in mine.

Finally, I would like to thank and acknowledge my wife, Yvette, for her abiding love, encouragement, and support. She prayerfully and patiently talked through concepts with me, read every chapter, and at times said, "Ah, not so much," so that I could make the concepts in this book better and more understandable and actionable. The Bible says he who finds a wife finds what is good and receives favor from the Lord. My wife graciously proves the truth of this promise daily.

CHAPTER ONE

A CLARION CALL TO FATHERS

"He will turn the hearts of the fathers to their children, and the hearts of the children to their fathers; or else I will come and strike the land with a curse."

Malachi 4:6 (NIV 1984)

SEVERAL YEARS AGO, my wife, Yvette, had an experience with a friend that dramatically and forever shaped my understanding of the importance of fatherhood from a Christian perspective. My wife told me she had invited this friend, who was not a Christian, to have lunch with her. They were eating outdoors on a beautiful spring day, and my wife was inspired. So rather than saying her usual silent prayer, Yvette asked her friend if it was okay for her to pray for the meal that they would share. Without hesitation her friend said, "That's fine."

Yvette started her prayer by saying, "Dear heavenly Father ..." She thanked God not only for their food but for the sunshine, the ducks, the fresh air. When she finished, Yvette noticed that her friend had a troubled look on her face. Fearing she had offended her friend, Yvette asked if there was something wrong with the prayer. Her friend paused for a moment and then said, "Oh, no. The prayer was fine. But I could never think of God as a heavenly father. My father was such an [#%&%*&!!]!"

When my wife told me this story, it really impressed upon me how the relationships people have with their earthly fathers have a direct and lasting impact on their ability to relate to God as Father. Indeed, it's understandable that the notion of a loving heavenly Father can have no meaning to those who have never experienced the love of their earthly father. In fact, if one's earthly father is so terrible, it would be easy to think a god who is a father might be infinitely terrible!

FATHERS: EARTHLY MIRRORS OF A HEAVENLY REALITY

The Bible says our struggle is not against flesh and blood, but against the powers of this dark world and against the spiritual forces of evil in the heavenly realms (Eph. 6:12). Over the years, God has shown me that the attack on the institution of fatherhood and the strategy to make fathers unloving and ineffective is a primary goal of Satan himself. Why? Because if fathers are distant, distracted, disconnected, or even abusive, children will believe all fathers are this way, even a heavenly Father who claims to love them unconditionally.

But this is clearly not God's plan. His desire is for all fathers to reflect aspects of his character, an earthly mirror of a heavenly reality. Matthew 7:9–11 illustrates this quite clearly. In this passage, Jesus is speaking to a group that must have included many fathers. Note what he says:

"Which of you, if your son asks for bread, will give him a stone? Or if he asks for a fish, will give him a snake? If you, then, though you are evil, know how to give good gifts to your children, how much more will your Father in heaven give good gifts to those who ask him!"

From God's perspective, all fathers—even ones who are not Christians—are created to imitate his goodness. In fact, if this were not the case, the entire analogy Jesus used loses its meaning. You see, I believe good fathers are an example of common grace, like the life-giving rain which falls on the righteous and the wicked alike (Matt. 5:45).

But there is more. When you contemplate the symbolism in Jesus' examples in Matthew 7:9–11, a deeper meaning, especially for fathers, is evident. For example, consider the comparison of bread to a stone. Especially to a small child, a piece of bread and a small stone may look the same and feel the same. But they are not the same. Bread was, and remains today, a key source of physical life and sustenance, and it represents spiritual life as Christ's body, which was broken for the salvation of the world. A stone, especially in the time of Christ, could be a tool of destruction and death. Remember, stones were used to martyr Stephen.

Now consider the symbolism in the comparison of a fish to a serpent. The fish is a key symbol of the Christian faith. Of note, Jesus' first disciples were fishermen whom he transformed into "fishers of men." These men fervently shared the good news that salvation is available for all men. In contrast, the serpent is the symbol of the Evil One who seeks to thwart the gospel and lead humankind down a path of destruction and death.

What Jesus is saying in this passage is that fathers should make sure their children have both physical and spiritual life. Godly fathers are to provide a pathway and a connection to God's saving grace because when they give their children "good gifts," it makes it much easier for children to connect with a heavenly Father who gave the best gift of all—his Son, who died on a cross for their sins. So when their children hear, "Dear heavenly Father," it's winsome rather than worrisome.

THE TRUTH ABOUT CHURCH AND MEN

The truth is, men have a long way to go in becoming the spiritual leaders in this nation. In 2007, the Barna Group did a study exploring faith-related activities, commitments, and perspectives of fathers and mothers. The study found that Christian mothers outpaced fathers in terms of spiritual activities and commitment. In fact, the Barna survey examined twelve different elements of faith behavior and perspective. Mothers were distinct from fathers on eleven of the twelve factors. Mothers were more likely than fathers to say that they are absolutely committed to Christianity and to embrace a personal responsibility to share their faith in Jesus Christ with others. Moreover, mothers were also more religiously active and, in a typical week, they were more likely than fathers to attend church, pray, read the Bible, participate in a small group, and attend Sunday school. The only area in which both were equal was in willingness to volunteer at a church. David Kinnaman, president of the Barna Group, says it all:

> Whether they are a parent or not, women in America have high levels of spiritual sensitivity and engagement. Men generally lag behind the spirituality of women—and particularly so if they

are not a father [sic]. In other words, having children intensifies the spiritual commitment of men, but even so most fathers still do not measure up to the spiritual footprint of their parenting counterparts.[1]

The bottom line is that we have a major problem here. Fathers have demonstrated that they are less likely to be spiritual to begin with, and yet if fathers are to be effective leaders for their families, they need to be sitting in the pews with them.

Several years ago *Touchstone* magazine published a thought-provoking article by Robbie Low called "The Truth about Church and Men" that further illustrates the link between fatherhood and saving grace. In the article, Low examined data from a Swiss national survey that sought to determine if a person's religion carried through to the next generations and if so, why, and if not, why not. Low concluded: "The result is dynamite. There is one critical factor. It's overwhelming, and it is this: It is the religious practice of the father of the family."[2] The survey data indicated the following:

If both father and mother attend regularly, 33 percent of their children regularly attend church and 41 percent attend irregularly. Only 25 percent don't attend at all.

If the father attends irregularly and the mother regularly, only 3 percent of the children attend church regularly, and 59 percent attend irregularly. And 38 percent don't attend at all.

If the father doesn't attend church and the mother attends regularly, only 2 percent of the children attend regularly, while 37 percent attend irregularly. Over 60 percent of the children don't attend church.

If the father attends regularly and the mother is irregular or non-practicing, 38 percent of children attend when the mother attends irregularly, and 44 percent of children whose mothers are non-practicing attend regularly.

These data are striking and compelling. In short, if the father does not regularly attend church, only 1 child in 50 becomes a regular attender, even if the mother attends regularly. Moreover, if the father attends church regularly, regardless of what the mother does, between two-thirds and three-quarters of the children become churchgoers (regular and irregular). Even if the father is an irregular churchgoer, between a half and two-thirds of the children attend church regularly or irregularly. Although these findings are for Switzerland, I doubt you would get different results in the United States.

GETTING CHURCHES ENGAGED

Given the above statistics, it should be easy to understand why one of my most important objectives as president of National Fatherhood Initiative was to get the church fully engaged in turning the hearts of fathers to their children. After all, National Fatherhood Initiative's mission is to improve the well-being of children by making sure they have involved, responsible, and committed fathers. There must be a sense of urgency with this work because today one out of three children nationally—three out of five in the African American community—are growing up in father-absent homes.[3] These children are more at risk for a range of the most intractable social ills such as teen pregnancy, low academic performance, poverty, and crime.

Persuaded by these facts, I set out on a mission to meet as many key pastors as I could, trying to enlist them in combatting the spiritual and social impact on children and families when fathers are not engaged. The meetings generally began and ended the same way. As I began, I told them how I believe there were few things closer to the heart of God than making sure that children have good and godly fathers. Then I would share the impact uninvolved and absent fathers were having on our families and communities. They would nod approvingly and share how important they believed this issue was and, in some cases, how the presence or absence of their father impacted their lives. So far so good ...

But when I would ask specifically what they were doing in their churches or ministries to help men be the fathers God desires them to be, they did not have an active plan. Now, don't get me wrong. These churches usually had some form of men's ministry. However, when I probed regarding what the men's ministry was, I found that they did not have a specific and intentional plan to help men be better dads and equip them to improve their skills as fathers. None addressed the myriad of questions I presented.

- Were they helping dads understand their unique calling as Christian fathers?
  - Their biblical responsibilities
  - Their children's needs
  - How to stay connected to teenagers
- Were fathers in the church organized so that they can support one another?
  - New dads
  - Teen dads
- What outreach did the church have to fathers in the community?
- Were they helping incarcerated fathers to
  - Stay connected to his family while in prison?
  - Make the transition after he was released?

DADS NEED HELP!

These are very key questions, because the research shows that dads need a lot of help. For example, a few years ago, National Fatherhood Initiative did a comprehensive survey called *Pop's Culture: A National Survey of Dads' Attitudes about Fathering*. One of the key questions we asked these dads was how prepared they felt they were to be fathers. Nearly half of the fathers said they were not prepared. More troubling, when we asked these dads if they felt they were replaceable by the mother of their children or another man, over half said they were.[4]

Now, let this sink in for a moment. These were not guys who could be dads or would be dads. These were fathers with children in the home under the age of eighteen! Yet, despite these disturbing statistics, most Christians do very little to prepare for fatherhood, and most churches and men's ministries do very little to help fathers get the skills that they desperately need.

Moreover, National Fatherhood Initiative did another comprehensive survey called, *Mama Says: A National Survey of Mothers' Attitudes on Fathering*. These mothers were given a list of four common places that might offer support to fathers to help them be better dads, and they were asked to rate each as "very important," "fairly important," or "not important." Eighty percent of the mothers rated "churches and other communities of faith" as a "very important" place where they would expect fathers to get help, ahead of schools, community organizations, and the workplace. In fact, church was even the number one option for mothers who described themselves as "not very religious" or "not at all religious."[5] So it stands to reason that if churches were really to embrace the call to help men be better dads, mothers inside and outside of the congregation would be supporting this effort.

In any case, after having lots of conversations with pastors, men's ministry leaders, and Christian dads, God gave me an insight about what was going on. I believe there is a shared perspective and misconception that if we can just help men be better Christians, they will automatically be better dads. In other words, good Christian men equals good Christian fathers. I must admit that this seems logical.

But here's the problem. When I started to examine the lives of so many men whose stories are chronicled in the Bible, I detected a disturbing pattern. Many of them, even men who had deep and abiding hearts for God, had made some rather serious mistakes as fathers that often impacted generations. Therefore, if these fathers had problems, why wouldn't fathers today? In fact, I believe this is why God made sure that these "bad dad" mistakes were front and center, consequences and all, in so many of the biblical narratives. God truly loves fatherhood and fathers, and he wanted these mistakes to be easy to find.

That is why I wrote this book. I am hopeful that as you study the examples of the fatherhood legacies of men like Abraham, David, and Eli—men who loved God deeply—you will learn from their mistakes. More importantly, my prayer for you is that this book will serve as a clarion call for you to take action now to be the father that God designed you to be. I am also hopeful you will make the "Good Dad Promise" at the end of each chapter to your wife (or the mother of your children) and your children, so you can leave a better fatherhood legacy than the ones that some of these fathers did. There is a saying that a wise man learns from his mistakes. This is true. But the *wiser* man learns from the mistakes of *others*.

BAD
DAD

MISTAKE #1

CHAPTER TWO

DAVID

HE WAS PARALYZED
BY HIS PAST FAILURES

Therefore, if anyone is in Christ, he is a new creation; the old
has gone, the new has come!

2 Corinthians 5:17 (NIV 1984)

WHEN I WAS TWENTY YEARS OLD, I did something that
no Christian young man is supposed to do. I got my girlfriend
Yvette pregnant. I can still remember, as if it was yesterday, the
moment I received the phone call from her to give me the news.
She was crying. She was confused. And she was terrified, because
she knew that she would have to tell her father, who had not quite
embraced the idea of my dating his daughter. Plus, since her body
would change and become a public reminder of our sin, she would
be ashamed and embarrassed.

I too was shaken, but mostly, I was disappointed in myself.
Because of my lack of self-control, I put the woman whom I
loved in a difficult situation. I had let her down. I had let my
family down. Most importantly, I had let God down, because I
knew well his principles of sexual purity, and I also knew well the

possible consequences of violating them. You see, my father had gotten my mother pregnant when he was about nineteen years old and she was about sixteen years old. Although they married and remained so for a few years, eventually they split up. My father, like too many others, became distant and disconnected from my life, leaving my mother to raise four small children on her own. So, early on, I vowed to not repeat my father's mistake.

Truth be told, I also felt like a hypocrite, and of course, I was one. I was a Christian, and most of my friends knew it. I went to church and Bible study regularly. I was even a member of the university's gospel choir. In fact, I used to be teased a bit because I proudly carried a big red Bible that I received in high school. I didn't really "lord" my faith over people, but I certainly wasn't shy about it either. So the fact that I got someone pregnant was a bit ironic, especially given that I had some friends who were clearly more sexually active than I was. Somehow, it just didn't seem fair. But actions—all actions—have consequences, and although you can control your actions, you can't control the consequences of your actions. This was a hard lesson to learn—one I am still challenged daily never to forget. So I determined to do the right thing. After a few months, Yvette and I got married and had our first son, Jamin. A few years later, we had our second son, Justin.

As my boys grew, I was on a mission to break the cycle of teen fatherhood. So when they were young, I would be sure to share and reinforce the biblical principle of saving sex for marriage. It was really easy then because they were more interested in the Dallas Cowboys than their cheerleaders and Hershey kisses than girl kisses. But I knew that this would change, and this made me nervous.

You see, in a sense, I was haunted by my past and how my first son was conceived. Therefore, as the time approached for me to have "the talk" with Jamin, I began to worry about how my son would deal with the news that his father had violated a principle that he had stressed for as long as he could remember. I feared that, even if he respected me too much to say it, he would think that I was a hypocrite. Every time I thought about this, I was paralyzed, so much so that at times I was tempted not to have "the talk" at all. But by the grace of God I did, and the conversations with both of my sons went well. I was very candid about my mistake and my hope and prayer that they would break the cycle of teen fatherhood in our family. The blessing was that they both did.

Over the years, as I have reflected on my dilemma, I realized that I was laboring under a misunderstanding that has plagued many fathers. I believe they struggle with understanding the difference between hypocrisy and spiritual growth. You see, hypocrisy is when you try to stop your children from doing something that you are currently doing. For example, when a father says, "Do as I say but not as I do." So if you try to admonish your children to stop doing something that is immoral or illegal while you continue to do so, you are being a hypocrite. And most likely your kids (and your wife) will call you on it.

However, spiritual growth is telling your children to not do something you did, because you learned it was not God's best for you or violated his principles. This is like a father saying, "Once I was blind, but now I see." Indeed, a blind man who receives his sight and helps others avoid a dangerous ditch that he once stumbled into is not a hypocrite. He's a hero. So too is the father who protects his children from repeating mistakes he made in the past.

There is a "bad dad" example in the life of David which clearly demonstrates how badly things can go when a father allows his past to paralyze him. Despite being a man after God's heart, David's family was not immune from the consequences of his failure to act.

SOWING SEEDS OF DYSFUNCTION

You have probably heard sermons about the struggle that David had with his third son, Absalom, who developed a hatred for his father that was so intense that he not only wanted to take David's kingdom, but also his life. Most people focus on the narrative of their destructive conflict. However, I think it's also essential to examine how the pernicious seeds of dysfunction were sown which ultimately choked the life out of their father-son relationship and ultimately caused so much pain in David's family.

In 2 Samuel 13, you will find that David's first son, Amnon, fell madly in love with his beautiful half-sister Tamar, whose brother was Absalom. Apparently, Amnon was having so much trouble trying to gain Tamar's affection that he became "frustrated to the point of illness." (Now that's lovesick!) In any case, one of Amnon's "shrewd" cousins concocted a plan that he should go to bed and pretend to be ill. When David inquired about Amnon, Amnon should ask for Tamar to come and nurse him back to health. Well, all went as planned, and Tamar was sent to Amnon's room.

After Tamar prepared some bread for Amnon, he requested that everyone except Tamar leave the room. Once they were alone, he asked Tamar to come to his bedroom to feed him. However, it became clear that Amnon was not planning to live by bread alone. He wanted Tamar to have sex with him. Tamar refused, but despite her pleading with him and suggesting that he simply ask David for her hand in marriage, Amnon wouldn't be denied. He raped his sister. To make matters worse, once Amnon got what he wanted, he essentially threw her away. He told his servant, "Get this woman out of here," and the servant put her out and bolted the door.

As you can imagine, Tamar was disgraced and cried inconsolably. She knew that since she was no longer a virgin, any hope for marriage and a family was essentially over. Her brother Absalom found her in this condition and asked, "Has Amnon, your brother, been with you?" So Absalom consoled her and had her live with him. It's worth noting that Absalom has a special love for his sister, so much so, that he named his daughter Tamar. In any case, it doesn't sound like Tamar ever recovered, because the Bible said that she lived as a "desolate woman" (v. 20).

Absalom never confronted Amnon about what he did to Tamar, but the Bible is very clear that Absalom hated him. Interestingly, when David found out what Amnon had done, he was furious, but he took no action to make things right, even though he knew that the law required a man who raped a virgin to marry her and never divorce her.

Well, two years later, Absalom came up with a plan to get revenge. He pretended that he wanted Amnon to go with him to see his sheepshearers and got David to approve the trip. However, Absalom had very different intentions. He told his men to wait until Amnon got drunk, and then they were to kill him, which they did. The old saying that "time heals all wounds" was certainly not the case in this situation, because since the day Amnon raped Tamar, Absalom's express intention was to kill Amnon. In any case, after the murder, Absalom fled to go and live with his maternal grandfather.

Now David had lost his oldest son. And soon, he would lose another son, because in a few years, Absalom would be killed after a failed conspiracy to take David's throne. In addition, he lost his daughter Tamar, who was emotionally destroyed. Also, I suspect that the mothers of Amnon, Absalom, and Tamar were very upset with David because he failed to take action to resolve the festering conflict. Indeed, David paid a very heavy price for inaction. So, one has to ask, "Why did he allow this to happen?"

PARALYZED BY HIS PAST

The Bible does not give us much detail, but I believe that we can get insight into why David failed to act by examining his past. You see, David had sinned like Amnon when he committed adultery with Bathsheba. He too used his power to take a woman who did not belong to him. Although he didn't rape her, he did something worse. He arranged to have her husband, Uriah, killed to cover up his sin.

It is very likely that Amnon, and all of David's family, knew about his sin with Bathsheba. I believe David was reluctant to take action with Amnon because he feared that Amnon, and possibly others, would accuse him of being a hypocrite. I can just see Satan, the accuser, whispering into David's ear, "David, you, of all people, are in no position to pass judgment on anyone. Shouldn't you be dead because of your sin? You hypocrite!" You see, the same passage in Deuteronomy that required a man who raped a virgin to marry her also said that a man who slept with another man's wife was to die.

I believe David was paralyzed by his past.

But he should not have been. Why? Because David had truly repented for his sin with Bathsheba. When the prophet Nathan confronted him, David said, "I have sinned against the Lord." And God, who is the final judge and arbiter, told David that he was not going to die for his sin of adultery. Moreover, David did not continue in this type of sin. He grew spiritually from the experience. Indeed, David wrote Psalm 51 as a sincere and beautiful act of contrition. Consider what he said in verses 3–4:

> For I know my transgressions,
>   and my sin is always before me.
> Against you, you only, have I sinned
>   and done what is evil in your sight;
> so you are right in your verdict
> and justified when you judge.

Unfortunately, I have seen too many situations where fathers have acted the way that David did because of their own past sins and transgressions. For example, I once talked to a father who said that he could not tell his daughter not to use drugs because he did drugs when he was a teen. In addition, there are countless dads who won't speak into the sexual lives of their children because of their sexual behavior in the past, even though the research shows that children with involved fathers are less likely to become sexually active.

Inaction is a mistake, but it's part of Satan's plan to destroy a family, just as he did in David's case. Indeed, it is critical that fathers not become paralyzed. God requires good dads to take action. After all, the physical, emotional, and spiritual well-being of their children is at stake.

REFLECTION: THINK ON THESE THINGS
Romans 3:23 tells us that we all have sinned and fallen short of the glory of God. Therefore, it is a natural aspect of the human condition for any father to have things in his past that he regrets.

However, the good news is that if we confess our sins, God is faithful and just and he will forgive us and cleanse us from all unrighteousness (1 John 1:9). In other words, when we truly confess, God presses the "reset button" and gives us a new beginning. The key is for us to accept God's forgiveness and move forward with our lives. If you are struggling with your past and accepting God's forgiveness, spend some time reflecting on the verses below. Don't give Satan a "stun gun" that can stop you from taking action with your children.

- In him we have redemption through his blood, the forgiveness of sins, in accordance with the riches of God's grace that he lavished on us. (Eph. 1:7–8)
- When we were overwhelmed by sins, you forgave our transgressions. (Ps. 65:3)
- I write to you, fathers, because you know him who is from the beginning. I write to you, young men, because you are strong, and the word of God lives in you, and you have overcome the evil one. (1 John 2:14)

CORRECTION: CHANGE THESE THINGS

When David found out that Amnon had raped his sister Tamar, he was furious, but unfortunately, he didn't take any action to correct the situation and make things right. Instead, he took the "ostrich" approach to fathering and just stuck his head into the sand, hoping that the situation would go away. However, the ostrich strategy doesn't stop danger and problems from coming. It just limits your ability to see them coming and proactively respond.

Are there problems and conflicts that have been brewing in your home that you are avoiding in hope that they will go away?

If so, now is the time to address them and to take action. Spend a few minutes prayerfully listing the problems and considering what actions you should take to address them.

CONNECTION: DO THIS THING

Now that you have reflected upon what God needs you to do regarding past mistakes and you have identified what you need to correct, it is time for you to make the Good Dad Promise. You need to make this promise to God, to yourself, to your wife (or the mother of your children), and to your children.

GOOD DAD

PROMISE #1

I will not be paralyzed by my past failures.

BAD DAD

MISTAKE #2

CHAPTER THREE

LABAN

HE MADE HIS CHILDREN COMPETE FOR HIS AFFECTION

Love does not delight in evil but rejoices with the truth. It always protects, always trusts, always hopes, always perseveres.

1 Corinthians 13:6–7

IN 2005, SINGER-SONGWRITER JOHN MAYER won the "Song of the Year" Grammy for a song called "Daughters." In the song, Mayer tells of a confusing relationship problem he is having with a woman with whom he is madly in love. You see, despite his best intentions and his offering his heart to her, he just can't seem to get close to her. She's afraid to be vulnerable, and there can be no true intimacy without vulnerability. Then Mayer has an epiphany ... an "ah-ha" moment. He realizes that this woman's problem is not about him. She has "daddy issues" from a father who left her life years ago.

Mayer is a very gifted songwriter, so it would be easy to conclude that he just came up with a catchy tune to pull heartstrings and sell records, especially to his millions of adoring female fans. But it turns out that this song is autobiographical. Note how he

41

explained his inspiration for writing "Daughters" a few years ago during a performance on the *VH1 Storytellers* show:

> "[I] loved a girl a lot ... but she couldn't trust men. If you traced it back as to why, [it was] the first man in her life that she couldn't trust.... I tried to figure out how I could possibly love this person, and the answer is you can't, because someone else didn't before you.... If I meet one more beautiful woman with daddy issues, I am going to go insane ..."[1]

Now, Mayer has had his share of tumultuous relationships with high-profile celebrity women and on occasion has said some very inappropriate things. But even though Mayer may not be the best messenger, there is a profound truth in his message. And it's clear that he really struck a chord with this song. Ironically, he said more in a couple hundred words than some fatherhood books I've read have said in a couple hundred pages. In fact, when I visited a website to watch a video of him performing the song, I was amazed by the impact of his song and by the comments posted by some of the women.

Here are just a few:

> "This song is so emotional for me. I cried the first time I heard it."
>
> "My father had to leave me when I was 6; I saw him again when I was 19, and was friends with him until he died when I was 28 ... nevertheless, there was a hole in my being."
>
> "This reminds me of my dad; he left ... actually, I don't know when he left, but I know he is out there somewhere and I hope someday I will find him to ask him why he left."

"This song describes me. My dad isn't really there for me."

The above posts are filled with emotion, hurt, longing, and uncertainty. The writers long for an important love that was lost and a connection that was never made but is still very much needed. However, all of the posts didn't have this tone. One woman wrote that she hated her father and that he "needed to listen to this song." I was saddened to learn that she was just a teen and that her favorite song is "I Hate You" by a group aptly named the Sick Puppies.

Much of the emphasis on the importance of fathers is focused on boys—and rightfully so. It's difficult to be what you don't see. So if boys don't see good dads who love them, their mothers, and their families, it's more difficult for them to grow up to be dads who do these things. Nonetheless, as the comments of the women and the teenage girl above reflect, fathers play an enormously important role in their lives as well. Their pain as women now is very much connected to their pain as little girls years ago.

Several years ago I had an opportunity to spend time with author Jonetta Rose Barras, who wrote *Whatever Happened to Daddy's Little Girl?: The Impact of Fatherlessness on Black Women*. By the time she was eight years old, Jonetta had lost three fathers—her biological dad as well as two other men who stepped into a father-figure role. Jonetta was inspired to write her book to help fathers truly understand the impact of their absence and to help the daughters heal. Note what she says about her own experience:

> A girl abandoned by the first man in her life forever entertains powerful feelings of being unworthy or incapable of receiving any man's love. Even when she receives love from another, she is constantly and intensely fearful of losing it. This is the anxiety,

the pain of losing one father. I had had three fathers toss me aside; the cumulative effect was catastrophic.[2]

Jonetta's words powerfully express a truism that I have seen firsthand in my family and over the years as president of National Fatherhood Initiative. In fact, if I had a quarter for every woman who has approached me to discuss her "daddy issues," I would be writing a book on how to manage your stocks rather than one to help dads build better bonds with their children!

You see, I learned a long time ago that a father plays a special role in a daughter's life, particularly when it comes to helping her trust and accept unconditional love. When things go as designed, he is the first man to pursue his daughter's heart. However, the key is that, unlike some guys she will meet, a good dad will pursue his daughter's heart in *her* best interest.

A good father gives her the security and confidence to know and believe that she is "love worthy" by the opposite sex. By his words and deeds, a good father shows his daughter at an early age what true love should feel like, instilling self-assurance that there can be safety in vulnerability and, most importantly, that she can find her "prince" without kissing all of the frogs! She won't reject the right guy or embrace the wrong guy out of fear.

That said, another very important point is expressed in "Daughters." The song's chorus reminds fathers that daughters will love like they are loved. In other words, fathers teach their daughters how to love and how not to love. So what lesson does a daughter learn about love when her father betrays her or leaves her vulnerable? And what does she learn when she has to compete for her father's love and affection? As we find from a study of the "bad dad" behavior of Laban, daughters will learn lessons that can have devastating and lasting consequences for generations.

LABAN AND HIS TWO DAUGHTERS

Most of the stories about families in the Bible focus on the relationship between fathers and sons. This is one of the reasons that I find the story of Laban to be a very special, important, and instructive one for fathers. In Genesis 29, we learn that Laban had two daughters, Leah and Rachel. Leah, the elder daughter, was not the most attractive one. She had weak eyes, while Rachel had a lovely figure and was beautiful.

One day, Laban's nephew Jacob arrived for a visit. The instant he saw Rachel he was smitten and wanted to marry her. So he and Laban worked out a deal. In order for Jacob to marry Rachel, he would have to work for Laban for seven years. So Jacob worked hard like any love-struck man would and kept his end of the bargain. But Laban did not. On the wedding night, he tricked Jacob and switched Leah for Rachel.

As you can imagine, when Jacob found out that he was now married to "weak eyes," he was livid. But Laban told him that it was customary for the older sister to be married before the younger one. However, to assuage Jacob, Laban offered him a special deal. All he needed to do was work another seven years and Laban would give him Rachel as a wife as well. So Jacob agreed. He worked seven more years and married Rachel, and everyone lived happily ever after. Well, not quite ... As the saying goes, "Hell hath no fury like a woman scorned." And due to Laban's trick, Jacob had just married two women who would bring a fury into his home for which he was not prepared.

A WOMB WAR

Alas, Jacob soon found out that there was not going to be much "honey" in his honeymoon with Rachel, because Leah and Rachel quickly started to compete for Jacob's love and attention. In fact, they launched a "womb war" that sowed seeds of family conflict and dysfunction for generations to come. Leah "struck" first and quickly gave Jacob four sons. It's worth noting that Leah, not Jacob, named all of their sons. The names she chose clearly indicated that she knew she was number two in Jacob's heart, but she deeply longed to earn his affections. In fact, after the birth of her third son Levi, whose name in Hebrew meant "joined," Leah said, "Now at last my husband will become attached to me, because I have borne him three sons" (Gen. 29:34).

Well, when Rachel failed to conceive, she became very jealous of her sister. She even began to blame Jacob, and told him, "Give me children, or I'll die" (Gen. 30:1). Desperate not to be outdone by her sister, Rachel eventually demanded that Jacob sleep with one of her maidservants so that she could have a family through Bilhah. When Jacob had the first son through the maidservant, Rachel took the victory with, "God has vindicated me," naming him Dan (v. 6). Of course, Leah then came back with a counterpunch, giving her maidservant to Jacob to bear children on her behalf.

At one point, these two competitive sisters even involved their children. One day, Leah's son Reuben found some mandrake fruits and gave them to his mother. Now, the mandrake was not just any fruit. It was actually called the "love apple" because it was thought to be an aphrodisiac that enhanced fertility. When Rachel found out about Reuben's mandrakes, she must have believed this was her sister's secret fertility weapon, because she demanded that Leah share. Leah retorted, "Wasn't it enough that you took away my husband? Will you take my son's mandrakes too?" (v. 15). Ouch.

46

Interestingly, similar to Jacob and Laban's negotiations, the sisters struck a win-win deal. Leah gave Rachel some of the mandrakes in exchange for an extra night to sleep with Jacob. Demonstrating just how bizarre and dysfunctional this situation had become, Leah went to Jacob and told him, "You must sleep with me. I have *hired* you with my son's mandrakes" (v. 16, emphasis mine). What a mess!

It's worth noting that the sibling competition did not end with Leah and Rachel. Since they modeled this destructive behavior for their sons, who became the twelve tribes of Israel, it continued for generations. The most notable example is reflected in the story of how Leah's sons conspired to sell Rachel's son Joseph — Jacob's favorite son — into slavery. (We will revisit this troubling story in chapter 4.)

LABAN, THE MANIPULATOR

Returning to Leah and Rachel, it's pretty easy to see how Laban's behavior and example played a substantial role in their conflict. After all, he selfishly set up the dynamic, which caused his daughters to compete for Jacob's love and affection. Although the Bible doesn't give much detail, I believe that Leah and Rachel learned from their father that love was not something that you get because of who you are; it was something that you earn because of what you do. After all, this is how Laban treated Jacob. Accordingly, could it not be how he had treated his daughters from the time they were small girls?

People tend to behave in a manner consistent with their character. In Laban's case, a key aspect of his character was his willingness to manipulate others to get what he wanted. My sense is that the way he treated Leah and Rachel during the situation with Jacob was not unusual; he may have often manipulated his daughters to compete against each other to suit his purposes and in contest for his love and affection.

The Bible does not give information about what Laban said to his daughters prior to tricking Jacob. Although Rachel may have been unaware of Laban's plan, Leah must have known what was going on. In fact, it's not hard to imagine a conversation where Laban tells Leah how going along with Daddy's plan and marrying Jacob is in her best interest. I suspect Laban knew that "weak-eyed" Leah had felt inferior to her younger, more beautiful sister for years, and as a manipulative father, he assuredly tapped into this insecurity. It would not have taken much for him to convince her that she was entitled to marry Jacob. After all, this might be her only chance to get married.

No doubt Rachel was devastated when she learned that Leah had married Jacob. But perhaps Laban stoked her competitive nature by suggesting that it was all Leah's idea in the first place. He may have said that he was all for her marrying Jacob, but Leah had reminded him of the custom that the older sister must marry first. Alas, his hands were tied by tradition. I bet Rachel thought, "That conniving Leah! She knows full well how much I love Jacob. She can't find her own husband, so she has to steal mine!"

Alas, it's clear that Laban did not love his daughters. You see, like marriage, fatherhood is a covenant relationship where the goal is to sacrificially give of yourself for another. So, although Laban was not physically absent, he was emotionally absent and disconnected at the heart from Leah and Rachel, which was just as painful. Unfortunately, Laban's relationship with Leah and Rachel was transactional—like a business deal—about what he could get from being their father. And business, by its very nature, is competitive. Therefore, it's not surprising that Laban's behavior sowed the seeds and weeds of competition and dysfunction into his family.

LOVE, GOD'S WAY

Laban's "bad dad" example is a cautionary one for fathers today. Even if it is not a father's plan to play favorites, the natural desire of children to please and be loved engenders competition. A home environment can become a battlefield where children feel that they must compete for love, affection, or esteem. But this is not God's plan. Love by its very nature is not supposed to be a competitive sport. Rather, it is sacrificial, as Christ consistently demonstrated in his life and then, finally, on the cross. Therefore, fathers who strive to imitate this example must always remember that every child is a unique blessing from God, "fearfully and wonderfully" made in God's image to be loved, affirmed, and valued, not for what they do or what they can do for you, but for who they are.

Long before John Mayer wrote the words to his song, the apostle Paul penned wonderful words that clearly expressed our heavenly Father's view of what true love must look like for our children. In 1 Corinthians 13:4–7, Paul wrote:

> Love is patient, love is kind. It does not envy, it does not boast,
> it is not proud. It does not dishonor others, it is not self-seeking,
> it is not easily angered, it keeps no record of wrongs. Love does
> not delight in evil but rejoices with the truth. It always protects,
> always trusts, always hopes, always perseveres.

Laban clearly strayed far from this model of true love, and it's sad that his daughters, as well as future generations, had to suffer the consequences of his "bad dad" behavior. However, the good news is that a tremendous and blessed legacy awaits fathers who model Paul's "love language." God will reward them with daughters and sons who will love like they do.

REFLECTION: THINK ON THESE THINGS

Take a moment to read 1 Corinthians 13. In this chapter, Paul gives us an excellent description of what love should look like from God's perspective. Love is certainly not a self-centered, competitive sport, like Laban and then his daughters made it, but rather, it is an other-centered reflection of sincere compassion and genuine caring. Indeed, real love is not about what you can get from others. It's about what you can give. In fact, Paul makes the point that love is the most important and lasting gift that you can give to anyone. This is why it is critically important that fathers be loving and model loving behavior for their children.

CORRECTION: CHANGE THESE THINGS

Look again at 1 Corinthians 13:4–7:

> Love is patient, love is kind. It does not envy, it does not boast, it is not proud. It does not dishonor others, it is not self-seeking, it is not easily angered, it keeps no record of wrongs. Love does not delight in evil but rejoices with the truth. It always protects, always trusts, always hopes, always perseveres.

The challenge for every dad is to truly examine his heart and his behavior to honestly determine if this is the type of love that he has been modeling for his children. A great exercise to help you assess how you are doing is to replace the words *love* and *it* in the passage above with the word *Dad*. When you do this, what specific areas have been most challenging for you? What aspects of your fathering do you need to change now?

CONNECTION: DO THIS THING

Now that you have reflected upon what God needs you to do, make sure that your children are not competing for your love and affection. Having identified what you need to correct, it's time for you to make the Good Dad Promise. You need to make this promise to God, to yourself, to your wife (or the mother of your children), and to your children.

GOOD DAD

PROMISE #2

I will not make my children compete for my affection.

BAD DAD

MISTAKE #3

CHAPTER FOUR

JACOB

HE TURNED A BLIND EYE TO SIBLING RIVALRY

What causes fights and quarrels among you? Don't they come from your desires that battle within you? You desire but do not have, so you kill. You covet but you cannot get what you want, so you quarrel and fight. You do not have because you do not ask God. When you ask, you do not receive, because you ask with wrong motives, that you may spend what you get on your pleasures.

James 4:1–3

MANY YEARS AGO, when my wife and I were new parents, we visited a couple that had two sons a bit older than ours. After introducing us to their boys, they took them to their play area in an adjacent room, so that we could talk without being interrupted. Well, not long after they closed the playroom door, these boys started going after each other. It sounded a bit like an Ultimate Fighting Championship® cage match. You could hear one son scream, "He's hitting me," and then lots of crying. Frankly, all that was missing from the scene was the famed boxing announcer

Michael Buffer exclaiming, "Let's get ready to rumble!" and a bell clanging to designate the start of another round.

Oddly, while this commotion was going on, the couple continued the conversation as if there was nothing wrong in the playroom. It was a bit surreal, like being in an earthquake with debris falling all around you, yet no one was running for shelter. Admittedly, I didn't know much about fathering at the time, but the whole situation seemed very peculiar to me, especially when I considered the father's reaction. Frankly, when this kind of thing happens, I would expect a father to excuse himself and go get his sons under control. But this father sat there totally unconcerned.

A few weeks later, we paid another visit to the home, and it felt like the movie *Groundhog Day*. We came in and sat down, their children were taken to the playroom, and again, the kids started going at each other. And again the father acted as if nothing was going on.

In fact, on a few occasions outside of the home, there were times when I would be talking with this father and his sons would be attacking each other. I certainly never doubted that he loved his boys, but he seemed to take a "no blood, no foul" approach to dealing with conflicts between them. At times I was tempted to step in and say something, but as the "junior" dad, I didn't feel I had the authority to do so. Nonetheless, this father's behavior made a significant impression on me. It caused me to vow to never let my boys treat each other this way, in private or in public. But observing this father's behavior also made me wonder why a dad would essentially turn a blind eye to sibling rivalry.

Over the years, we lost touch with this couple and their children, so I don't know how the relationship between his children developed. However, I know of plenty of situations where brothers and sisters harbor deep-seated anger and resentment because of unresolved childhood conflicts. In these cases, fathers, much like the one that I describe above, basically stood by under the misguided notion that their children would eventually "just figure this stuff out."

I have especially seen this type of passive fathering in situations where the fights between the children were verbal rather than physical. As I have thought about this over the years, it struck me that fathers who don't get involved in these instances believe two phrases often quoted that are fallacies. The first idiom heard frequently in schoolyards is "Sticks and stones may break my bones, but words will never hurt me." Now, of course, this is a fantastic retort for a ten-year-old who is being teased, but it's just not true.

In my role at National Fatherhood Initiative, I spend a lot of time talking with people about past hurts. In my experience, most people connect their woundedness and emotional pain to something that was said to them, especially as a child. Indeed, words can, and do, hurt a lot, and if a father allows his children to continually say hurtful things to each other, the consequences can be long-lasting. It can create insecurity and a poor self-image into adulthood. Remember, Philippians 4:8 says that our children should be thinking about things that are true, honorable, just, pure, lovely, commendable, excellent, and worthy of praise (ESV). Accordingly, to the best of his ability, a father should make sure the words his children hear from their siblings reflect the essence of this important verse.

The second idiom is "Time heals all wounds." Again, although this saying is quite poetic, it's just not true. My wife is a physician, and she would be quick to tell you there are many types of wounds that, if left untreated, are made *worse* by the passage of time. Alas, it's not time that heals wounds. Medicine and proper treatment do. I believe that the wounds siblings inflict on each other fall into this category. After all, those who should love you the most can hurt you the most. That's why God gave children fathers, who, like good physicians, can teach them how to apply the "medicines" of repentance when they have hurt their siblings and forgiveness when they have been hurt by their siblings.

But there is another critical reason I believe fathers must take a leadership role in stemming sibling rivalry. If not addressed, sibling rivalries can and do escalate into abuse and even violence. For example, in a story in *The New York Times* about sibling rivalry, Daniel Smith reflects on growing up with an abusive older brother. He said that he received beatings from his brother repeatedly from infancy up into his teens. His brother would grip him in a headlock or stranglehold and punch him repeatedly. He also said, "Fighting back just made it worse, so I'd just take it and wait for it to be over ... What was I going to do? Where was I going to go? I was 10 years old."[1] Sadly, one has to wonder where Daniel's father was while this was going on. In any case, it's not surprising that as a result of this abuse, Daniel and his brother were estranged for most of their adult lives.

But some children don't just "take it," as we learn from the sad tale of what happened between the Gorzynkski brothers. A few years ago, William Gorzynkski, age fifteen, and his younger brother Matthew, age fourteen, who lived with their father, were home alone. William wanted to watch TV, but his younger brother wanted to pump up the volume on his music. The brothers got into a heated argument that became physical and escalated into a fight. Matthew, who was the stronger and more athletic of the two, repeatedly started punching William in the head. The fight moved to the kitchen, where Matthew cornered William. Hoping to scare his brother and in a moment of panicked desperation, William grabbed a seven-inch kitchen knife. Unfortunately, he ended up stabbing his younger brother once in the chest. A shaken and remorseful William called 911 immediately and the paramedics arrived quickly, but they could not save Matthew. Consequently, William was arrested and charged with manslaughter.

The news reports stated the family was puzzled by how such a small conflict could turn tragic so quickly. After all, William's lawyer told the press, William and Matthew "fought like every other brothers do ..."[2] But maybe that is the problem. Could it be that if you examine the relationship these two brothers had, over time, you would find a trail of escalating arguments and physical fights? I doubt we will ever know. However, this case clearly shows the real physical, emotional, and spiritual consequences of unchecked sibling rivalry, and why dads must never turn a blind eye. Unfortunately, this "bad dad" mistake is an ancient one, as we will see when we examine how Jacob was affected by and contributed to significant sibling rivalry.

JACOB AND ESAU: INTENSE SIBLING RIVALRY

Before we take a look at where Jacob went wrong, it will be helpful to consider some history that certainly impacted his family dynamics. First, from the womb Jacob was involved in a very intense sibling rivalry with his older twin brother, Esau. You may recall that Jacob used his cooking skills to trick Esau into giving up his birthright for a bowl of lentil soup. Also, Jacob was clearly the favorite son of his mother Rebekah. With her help, he was able to trick his nearly blind father, Isaac, into giving him a blessing Isaac clearly desired to give to Esau. As you can imagine, Esau truly hated Jacob. And, given his deceptive ways, it's not surprising that Jacob, a guy who loved hanging with his mother in the kitchen, ended up having to run for his life from Esau, a guy who knew a thing or two about hunting prey.

Second, you may recall from a previous "bad dad" story that Jacob ran from one sibling rivalry mess to Laban's household, where he helped feed another sibling rivalry when he married sisters Leah and Rachel. Even though Rachel was the second wife, she was clearly Jacob's favorite. Significant conflict ensued between the sisters, in part because Rachel had difficulty conceiving, and Leah did not. Finally, after Leah had borne six sons, Rachel bore Jacob two sons, Joseph and Benjamin. If there was anyone who should have known a thing or two about the pernicious consequences of sibling rivalry, it should have been Jacob. Therefore, it is ironic that he handled his sons the way he did, especially Joseph.

JACOB LOVED JOSEPH MORE

We find the story of Joseph starting in Genesis chapter 37 when seventeen-year-old Joseph was out in the fields herding the family's flock with some of his brothers. The Bible doesn't indicate exactly what happened, but for some reason, Joseph gave his father a bad report about his brothers. The passage indicates the special relationship that Joseph and his father shared. Specifically, the Bible says Jacob loved Joseph more than any of his brothers, and that he demonstrated this extraordinary affection for Joseph by giving him a distinctive robe.

Now, let's pause here for a moment and consider what is going on.

If you have ever been around children, you know that one of the inviolable "kid laws" is not telling on one another. Those who violate it even earn a derogatory name. "Tattletales" are usually resented not just by the one who gets in trouble, but by all of the children because they know they could be the next victims.

It is clear Jacob made sure all of his sons knew Joseph was his favorite. I suspect that making a multicolored coat was no small task. By giving this very visible token of affection to Joseph, Jacob made a "bad dad" move that added fuel to an increasingly volatile situation between Joseph and his brothers. Undoubtedly one of the key causes of sibling rivalry is when children feel they are getting unequal amounts of attention and affection from their parents. In fact, a few years ago, I learned just how sensitive a child could be to such a slight.

I have two sons who are about two and half years apart in age. Well, a few years ago, my youngest son and I were down in our basement going through some old photos when we came across one from a time when I coached his older brother's youth baseball team. As I looked closely at the picture, I noticed something I had not seen before. Someone had taken a needle and put a small but noticeable X across my face. When I showed the photo to my son, who was twenty-four years old at that time, he sheepishly admitted he had done this to my picture when he was about seven years old because he was jealous that I was coaching his older brother's team. I had no idea he felt this way.

There is a bit of irony here. You see, my older son was clearly the best player on his team, and I was so sensitive about the appearance of favoritism that I was harder on my son than I should have been. Because I didn't think I handled the situation well with his older brother, I thought I would spare his brother the grief, so I purposely didn't coach my younger son's team the following year.

Interestingly, my younger son was more committed to athletics, even earning an NCAA Division 1 scholarship to play football. I spent more time working out with him than his older brother, who was less serious about sports. In the long run, I suspect he acknowledged this additional investment of my time as the reason I didn't coach his teams. But at the age of seven, before his own time had come, all he could see was the attention his older brother was getting. This situation certainly gives a glimpse into how Joseph's brothers may have felt slighted by the inequities.

There is another important aspect to consider regarding how Jacob treated Joseph compared to his brothers. By the time Joseph was seventeen years old, his mother Rachel was gone, having died giving birth to Benjamin. So it is very possible Jacob's oversized affection toward Joseph was a proxy for his love for Rachel, his favorite wife. No doubt he longed for her and missed her dearly. Nonetheless, the circumstances did not excuse his behavior. You see, it's always a "bad dad" mistake for a father to let something missing *in him* cause his children to miss something *from him*.

But there is another aspect that certainly impacted the growing animosity from Joseph's brothers: Jacob's relationship with his first wife, Leah. It's not hard to imagine that Leah, who for years had played second fiddle to Rachel, still harbored bitterness toward her sister. Although the Bible doesn't say more about the sisters' relationship, I would assume their relationship remained chilly at best. And then when Rachel died, Leah may have believed she would finally have Jacob's undivided love and affection. But with Jacob favoring Joseph over Leah's sons, I suspect her sibling rivalry continued with Rachel, even from the grave. As Jacob publicly demonstrated his love for Joseph, Leah may have received it as yet another painful rejection via her sons. Leah then may have helped to fan her sons' flames of resentment toward Joseph as a consequence.

BLIND TO CHARACTER FLAWS

You see, turning a blind eye to sibling rivalry often blinds a father to other family dynamics that need to be addressed as well. We certainly see this in Jacob's failure to address the growing jealousy of Joseph's brothers. But sibling rivalry can also blind a father to character flaws in his children, such as selfishness or lying, that often contribute to the rivalry. And I believe Jacob had a problem in this area as well when it came to his favorite son Joseph.

In Genesis 37:5–8, we learn that Joseph had a dream in which he and his brothers were working in a field binding sheaves. Joseph's sheaf arose and stood upright and his brothers' sheaves bowed down to his. Well, when Joseph told his brothers about his dream, they considered it more of a nightmare. They said, "Do you intend to reign over us? Will you actually rule us?" Not surprisingly, they hated him even more than before. To make matters worse, Joseph had a second dream in which the sun, the moon, and eleven stars bowed down to him. It doesn't take much interpretive skill to get the meaning of this dream. The imagery suggested that his father (the sun), his mother (the moon), and his eleven brothers (the stars) would bow down to him. When Joseph told his father and his brothers about this one, predictably, his brothers were jealous of him, and even Jacob rebuked him (Gen. 37:9–11).

When you consider what was happening here, a few important things stand out. First, it's pretty clear God was foreshadowing Joseph's destiny. However, the Bible does not say God instructed Joseph to share the content of his dreams with his brothers or even his father. Also, one could assume Joseph knew there was tension between him and his brothers. After all, boys will be boys. Nonetheless, if Joseph was clueless to this fact, after his brothers' response to the first dream, he should have had no doubt in his mind that they had animus toward him.

So, you have to ask yourself, why did Joseph share these dreams with his brothers? In my opinion, the answer is pretty clear. Young Joseph was a bit of a braggart, and he had a spirit of pride that was clearly contributing to the sibling rivalry. Alas, in many cases of sibling rivalry, the role of "victim" and "perpetrator" is often unclear, because there are complex family dynamics at play. So good dads must have godly wisdom if they are to handle these situations in the right way.

Interestingly, given Jacob's background, he was uniquely suited to help Joseph with his character flaws. As a young man, Jacob had similar character issues and a long history of being a deceiver. Remember, he had tricked his older brother Esau out of his birthright and fooled his blind and elderly father into giving him Esau's blessing. Also, Jacob knew well how to restore a good relationship with an angry and jealous brother. Genesis chapter 32 details the careful and thoughtful process Jacob used to reestablish his relationship with Esau. Jacob humbled himself and made restitution for the wrong that he had done.

In short, Jacob the deceiver had much that he could teach Joseph the braggart. Of note, the root causes of deception and bragging are pride and the desire to puff one's self up. In fact, these traits are pernicious evil twins. A deceiver fails to tell something that someone *should* know and a braggart tells someone something that they *shouldn't* know. Both the deceiver and the braggart seek to gain an advantage over others rather than do as the Bible says and consider others more highly than themselves. That's why God's antidote to cure both of these conditions is wisdom (knowing what is right) and humility (obediently doing what is right). Jacob had clearly learned this, but he missed a key opportunity to pass this important lesson on to young Joseph.

Well, eventually Joseph's brothers' jealousy and anger reached its tipping point, and they took action. On one occasion, Joseph's brothers were in a faraway pasture with their flock, and Jacob sent Joseph to check on them. When his brothers saw Joseph coming from afar, they conspired to kill him. Fortunately, his oldest brother Reuben's cooler head prevailed, and they decided to sell Joseph to a band of traveling merchants who took him to Egypt. Then his brothers took Joseph's prized multicolored coat, splattered it with goat's blood, and gave it to Jacob. They made their father believe a fierce animal killed his beloved son. As you can imagine, Jacob was inconsolable. Sibling rivalry often leaves fathers this way. It's painful when those you love the most hate each other.

Genesis chapters 39 through 41 chronicle the injustice, suffering, and harsh treatment Joseph experienced at the hands of many in Egypt. But the story does not end this way because, eventually, by God's grace, Joseph gets a chance to rise to power and fulfill his destiny. Indeed, what Joseph's brothers meant for evil, God used for good. That said, the good outcome for Joseph in no way absolves Jacob of his responsibility to proactively resolve his sons' conflict. In fact, ironically, Jacob's behavior may have caused God to remove Joseph from his care.

We all know God is sovereign and he will accomplish his purposes. However, I believe God would like to accomplish his purposes *through* us rather than *around* us. In the case of Joseph, God certainly knew he had some character issues that needed to be addressed, and he even gave Joseph the perfect father to help him develop the godly wisdom and humility that he would need to fulfill his destiny. But for a variety of reasons, Jacob made several "bad dad" mistakes and was blind to the actions he needed to take. So God removed Joseph from Jacob's presence for many years and used the trials in Egypt as a crucible to help Joseph refine his character. Although Jacob was eventually reunited with his son, he suffered a great deal and was never able to make up for the precious time they were apart. Alas, there are always painful consequences when a father fails to act.

You see, I believe God's desire is to use fathers to help accomplish his will through their children. That's why our heavenly Father entrusts earthly fathers with children in the first place. Good and godly fathers are to have foresight and insight when their children clearly lack it. But when a dad is unable or unwilling to do what needs to be done, God may choose to do it without him. And this fact, which Jacob's story illustrates, should be a sobering wake-up call for every dad.

REFLECTION: THINK ON THESE THINGS

In Genesis 48, when Jacob was near death, he called Joseph and his two sons to his bedside so he could bless Joseph's sons before he died. So Joseph did as his father requested. When it was time to give the blessings, Jacob stretched out his right hand and laid it on the head of Ephraim, who was the younger, and placed his left hand on the head of Manasseh, who was Joseph's firstborn. When Joseph saw what Jacob was doing, he tried to correct him by moving Jacob's right hand, which signified the blessing of the firstborn, onto his older son's head. But Jacob refused and told Joseph that although both sons would be great, his younger son would be the greater.

This passage is very interesting because it illustrates Joseph was acutely aware of the conflict and rivalry that could develop between his sons due to Jacob's actions. Alas, sibling rivalry had marred both his relationship with his brothers and Jacob's relationship with his brother Esau. And Joseph had the wisdom to not want to pass this legacy on to his sons. There is an old saying that those who forget the lessons of the past are destined to repeat them. Indeed, one of the strangest things in life is that, too often, we replicate that which we hate from our past.

Think about your children. Are there rivalries and quarrels among them? Reflect for a moment about your childhood and your relationships with your siblings. Were there quarrels among you? Are you allowing your children to repeat behavior from your past? If so, why?

CORRECTION: CHANGE THESE THINGS

Sibling rivalry is as old as Cain and Abel, and as a dad, you should expect to deal with this issue from time to time. That said, the key is to be prepared for it and also to make sure you are not contributing to the conflict. Below are a few of my suggestions along with some advice from experts to help your children get along better.

Don't play favorites.

Make sure that you don't compare your children to one another, even in fun.

Celebrate your children's individual talents and unique skills.

Never set your children up to compete with one another for your approval.

Be alert and proactive. Take note if there are particular activities or "triggers" that often lead to conflict. Do your best to plan for them and mitigate them.

Teach your children to positively encourage each other.

Help your children understand that there is a difference between being treated "fairly" and being treated "equally." As a dad, you should strive to treat your kids fairly.

Treat verbal conflicts just as seriously as physical ones. Words hurt and can leave lasting scars.

Remember to focus on the three T's (tongue, temper, and tone) when you are encouraging a child to apologize.[3]

If you are having an especially difficult challenge in this area, you may want to consider seeing a trained Christian counselor. In addition, you may want to read *Keep the Sibling, Lose the Rivalry: 10 Steps to Turn Your Kids into Teammates* by Dr. Todd Cartmell and *Peacemaking for Families* by Ken Sande and Tom Raabe.

CONNECTION: DO THIS THING

Now that you have reflected upon what God needs you to do to make sure that you don't turn a blind eye to sibling rivalry and you have identified what you need to correct, it's time for you to make the Good Dad Promise. You need to make this promise to God, to yourself, to your wife (or the mother of your children), and to your children.

GOOD DAD

PROMISE #3

I will not turn a blind eye to sibling rivalry.

BAD DAD

MISTAKE #4

CHAPTER FIVE

SAUL

HE MADE IT DIFFICULT FOR HIS CHILDREN TO HONOR HIM

Honor your father and your mother, so that you may live long in the land the LORD your God is giving you.

Exodus 20:12

ON THE NIGHT OF DECEMBER 10, 2008, the FBI received an especially strange call. Two brothers wanted to report a very serious crime. Hours before, their father, who ran an investment business that employed them, confessed to them that he was running a fraud of grand proportions, one that would go down in history as the largest ever committed. In fact, these brothers told the FBI that their father's business, despite its storied history, venerable reputation, and impressive client list, was nothing more than an elaborate Ponzi scheme, where a new investor's money simply was used to pay the expected returns of earlier investors. Now the gig was up, and their father had no choice but to come clean.[1]

Their father was Bernie Madoff, the now disgraced New York City financier. As the news reporters began to cover the Madoff story, I followed the details very closely because prior to becoming

75

president of National Fatherhood Initiative, I made my living as a registered investment advisor for Goldman Sachs, one of the nation's leading investment banking firms, where I managed investment portfolios for very wealthy people. Although I never had any dealings with Madoff's firm, I worked with and competed for business against other firms that had similar business models. These firms were typically a family affair, started by a father who dreamed of passing a successful business on to his children. Given my interest in fatherhood and my background in the investment business, I was an "easy mark" for a story like this.

One of the aspects of the story that I found most interesting was that Madoff's business was not a Ponzi scheme from the beginning, as is usually the case. Bernard L. Madoff Investment Securities, which he started in 1961 with just $200 in assets, had amassed a capital account of over $500,000 by 1969 and continued to grow rapidly.[2] He seemed to be blessed with a Midas touch. For example, despite long odds, Madoff boldly challenged the entrenched New York Stock Exchange traditional broker model by using aggressive marketing approaches to acquire key clients. He had superior networking and relationship-building skills.[3] In addition, Madoff had a keen eye for innovation and was one of the first to understand the tremendous potential of electronic trading technology, designing software that could trade stocks electronically in seconds.[4] He later became the chairman of this medium, known as NASDAQ. As Madoff's reputation grew, he was able to join all the right clubs and be a member of all the right circles. He became a much-sought-after advisor to super-wealthy and influential people, including even the regulators at the Securities and Exchange Commission.

Madoff certainly lived well, but he seemed to have a real sense that he also had an obligation to give back to others. Maybe this was due to his upbringing in a middle-class Queens neighbor-hood. Whatever the reason, Madoff became a very prominent philanthropist who could be counted on to give generously to causes ranging from the arts to education to cancer research. In addition, he served on numerous nonprofit boards.[5]

Madoff, who married his high school sweetheart Ruth in 1959, also took his role as a father quite seriously. So it's not surprising that he brought his two sons, Mark and Andy, into the firm very early in their business careers. The older son, Mark, who has been described as more easygoing and low-key, was responsible for the firm's trading business, while Andy immersed himself in the firm's technological issues and special projects. Madoff supported his sons financially, including giving them loans. It was pretty clear that the firm was Madoff's and his sons were the heirs apparent, with Mark, due to his superior people skills, likely positioned to eventually succeed his father as the head of the business. I think that this quote from an April 2009 *CNN Money* article says it all:

> There was no question that the Madoffs were the firm's royal family. Mark and Andy worked among their colleagues on the trading floor, but they sat on a raised platform, a few feet above everybody else. And even star employees knew that they could rise only so high.[6]

So, by all accounts, Madoff had it made. He was married to a woman whom he adored. He had prestige, esteem, and connections that most people could only dream about. And he had two sons who were positioned to successfully carry on his legacy and good name.

But something happened that would eventually lead to his downfall and destroy his family in the process.

The many compromises that ultimately lead to moral failure are a lot like beach erosion. They happen very gradually over time until the line between what you *won't* do and what you *will* do becomes almost imperceptible. Some cross the line because of greed. Others do so because of a fear of failure. And others do so to protect their reputation. In Madoff's case, it may have been a combination of these factors and others. We may never truly know. However, something happened that caused him to cross the line and start the fraud.

News reports indicated that at his trial he offered that the fraud started in the early 1990s, when he felt "compelled"[7] to give institutional investors strong returns despite the weak stock market and a national recession. He also told the court, "When I began the Ponzi scheme I believed it would end shortly and I would be able to extricate myself and my clients from the scheme. However, this proved difficult and ultimately impossible."[8] Indeed, it is ironic that the same man who would boast of personal interest on his website would end up scamming those closest to him:

> In an era of faceless organizations owned by other equally faceless organizations, Bernard L. Madoff Investment Securities LLC harks back to an earlier era in the financial world: The owner's name is on the door. Clients know that Bernard Madoff has a personal interest in maintaining the unblemished record of value, fair-dealing, and high ethical standards that has always been the firm's hallmark.[9]

Recently, someone told me there is an African saying about the child/parent relationship that goes: "I am who I am because you are who you are." And this made me think about what it must have been like for Mark and Andy Madoff to hear the father, whom they both loved and respected, tell them that the business that he built for them was "one big lie." The Madoff family is Jewish and certainly would be well-versed in the Ten Commandments, so the brothers knew well the fifth commandment that admonished them to honor their father. However, I suspect that they were tortured with a terrible conflict. How was a son to honor a father who had done such a dishonorable thing to them, their mother, their family, and the broader community? I wonder if Leviticus 19:32 came to mind, which says, "You shall stand up before the gray head and honor the face of an old man ..." (ESV).

Honor, which some may consider a quaint idea today, was a very important concept during biblical times. In a world that was based on oral communication, being an honorable man was critical, because your word had to be your bond. In fact, one Bible commentary asserted that honor, as the primary measure of social status, was based on two separate but interrelated constructs. Honor could either be *ascribed* or *acquired*.[10] For example, ascribed honor was given due to being part of a social unit like a family. This notion is reflected in the fifth commandment, since God ordained fathers to be honored based solely on their role. Similar to a king or ruler, this honor reflected the respect or esteem due or claimed by right. On the other hand, acquired honor is gained (or lost) by what one does. But these two forms of honor are truly connected, because if one does dishonorable acts in the public square, it will certainly impact someone's willingness to support or recognize the honor that is ascribed to you.

And this is why Madoff's confession to his sons must have been so difficult for them. As their father, he had God-ascribed honor. However, by his dishonorable acts, he had squandered not just his acquired honor but also theirs as well. You see, I believe that the fifth commandment is not just a one-sided command designed to get one's children to behave — under the threat of death. It is an implied command for fathers as well that presupposes that fathers would be worthy of honor. In short, in the fifth commandment, God linked ascribed honor to acquired honor to guide the behavior of fathers and their children. It's worth noting as well that when children honor their fathers, they are also honoring themselves, as the African proverb says, "I am who I am because you are who you are." Also, when children can't find anything honorable about their fathers, too often they will find something shameful about themselves. And this is what ultimately happened in the case of Mark, Madoff's oldest son.

A *Wall Street Journal* article reported on the problems that Mark Madoff encountered trying to find work in the financial services industry. Despite decades of experience and his considerable connections, no Wall Street firm would touch him. Proverb 22:1 says, "A good name is more desirable than riches; to be esteemed is better than silver and gold." Unfortunately, Mark's name was "Madoff," and in the minds of many, this name was now worthless and not worthy of honor, useful only as an expletive, an example of what one should not become or the punch line of a late-night comedian's joke.

A couple of weeks after this article, on the second anniversary of the scandal, Mark took his life in a dramatic fashion. He hung himself with a dog's leash from a ceiling pipe in his living room, while his toddler son slept in a nearby bedroom. No doubt, Mark Madoff had been deeply troubled ever since he turned his father over to law enforcement. Indeed, his dreadful end was yet another poignant example of how the sins of a father can impact his children and his grandchildren as well.

Since Mark's death, his brother Andy has done several interviews to discuss the impact of their father's crime on his brother and him. In an emotional *60 Minutes* segment, he said that in his family "we had a moral life with a clear sense of what's right and wrong."[11] Moreover, it has been very difficult for him to come to grips with the fact that for decades his father used his and his brother's legitimate trading business to hide his illegal activity. He offered that they were "human shields." He said, "I will never understand it. I will never speak to him again. I will never forgive him for it."[12] And it's clear that he will never honor his father again.

Indeed, there is an important lesson here that Bernie Madoff failed to learn. One of the most important gifts that a father can give to his children is not wealth but rather a life example that is worthy to be honored. One's honor is more easily kept than restored. But Madoff was not the first father who missed this lesson, as we will see by examining the relationship between Saul and Jonathan, his eldest son.

THE RIGHT MAN FOR THE JOB

The story of Saul enters the biblical narrative in 1 Samuel 8. The prophet Samuel, who also served as Israel's judge, was getting old, so he decided to designate his two sons to replace him as judge. Though, unfortunately, his sons "did not follow his ways," and the elders of Israel wanted to replace them, asking Samuel to appoint a king to rule over them. Samuel had some keen reservations about honoring their request, but after consulting with God, he set out on a quest to find the right man for the job.

When Saul is first mentioned in the text, his father Kish was about to send him on a quest to find some lost donkeys. (Now, this is certainly great training for anyone who might be a leader someday!) So Saul headed out on his journey with a servant. After he and his servant had traveled for some time into the land of

Zuph and had no luck finding the donkeys, Saul was ready to head home, lest his father get worried about him. However, his servant said to him, "Look, in this town there is a man of God; he is highly respected, and everything he says comes true. Let's go there now. Perhaps he will tell us what way to take" (1 Sam. 9:6). In other words, if anyone can help us find lost donkeys, a prophet can! But, despite the enticing suggestion, Saul was reluctant to go and meet the prophet because they didn't have a gift or offering to give Samuel. Fortunately, his servant had some money and they headed to the city.

Before Saul and his servant found Samuel, the Lord told him, "About this time tomorrow I will send you a man from the land of Benjamin. Anoint him ruler over my people Israel; he will deliver them from the hand of the Philistines. I have looked on my people, for their cry has reached me" (1 Sam. 9:16). Then, when Samuel caught sight of Saul, the Lord told him, "This is the man I spoke to you about; he will govern my people" (v. 17). Samuel immediately invited Saul to share a meal and declared, "And to whom is all the desire of Israel turned, if not to you and your whole family line?" (v. 20).

Well, Saul was taken aback. After all, he was merely a Benjamite, from the smallest tribe of Israel, and his clan was the least of all the clans of the tribe. Nonetheless, Saul shared the meal with Samuel. At this time, Samuel revealed God's plan that Saul was to be made king of Israel, and he told Saul to be on the lookout for several prophecies that would confirm his selection.

As Saul made his way home, each of the prophecies occurred, just as Samuel said. In fact, 1 Samuel 10:9 says that God "changed Saul's heart." Indeed, when Saul began to prophesy, it became clear to all who knew Saul that something had happened to him.

But when he reported back to his uncle, he said nothing about the fact that he would become king of Israel.

Shortly thereafter, Samuel called all of the tribes of Israel together and told them that God had answered their prayers and would give them a king. Samuel then cast lots, so that the people would clearly know that the man chosen was God's pick, not his. Tribes were eliminated and then men were eliminated until Saul was the only man left. However, when it was time to introduce Saul, he could not be found. God told them that Saul was hiding in the baggage. Saul could hide but he could not run. He was God's anointed one. So Samuel presented Saul, who was the tallest and most handsome man of all the people of Israel, as their king.

The biblical account of how Saul rose from obscurity to king gives us some insight into his character as a young man. Specifically, he seemed to have humility and an understanding of the importance of honor. For example, donkey chasing is certainly not the most glamorous of jobs for the most handsome guy in the land. However, he was humbly obedient and did as his father requested. When his servant suggested that they go see Samuel, he listened to a subordinate and was willing to heed his suggestion. In fact, his only concern was that they should have a gift to honor a prophet of Samuel's stature. And when Samuel spoke to Saul for the first time, Saul responded with humility and exclaimed that he was unworthy because his tribe and clan were the least of all. Also, when he met his uncle upon returning home, he certainly could have bragged that he was to be king, yet he said nothing. And when the lots were cast and he was officially chosen as king, he was not gloating. He was hiding. Finally, Saul held his tongue in the light of praise and ridicule, as the people showed their support by exclaiming "Long live the king!" followed by naysayers in his own town asking, "How can *this* fellow save us?" (1 Sam. 10:24, 27).

Much like Bernie Madoff, Saul was blessed with success early in his reign. For example, God gave him a quick and decisive victory over the Ammonites, who were a longstanding enemy of Israel. This success caused much excitement among the Israelites — so much so, that they officially established the kingdom with Saul as the head (1 Samuel 11).

KING SAUL'S KEY MISTAKES

Saul began to rule at age thirty and reigned till age seventy-two (1 Sam. 13:1). But it is very clear that, again like Madoff, Saul began to change over the long course of his reign. He made a number of key mistakes that eventually did great harm to his roles as king and father, moving him into "bad dad" territory.

Saul's first major mistake is recorded in 1 Samuel 13. He was in a battle with the Philistines, and after his son, Jonathan, defeated a garrison of Philistine troops, they responded by mustering a massive force of three thousand chariots, six thousand charioteers, and soldiers "as numerous as the sand on the seashore" (v. 5). Saul only had about three thousand troops, so he and his men headed for the caves to hide. The Bible actually says that these men were "quaking with fear" (v. 7).

However, it's clear from the passage that Saul must have sent word for Samuel to come and give an offering in order to gain God's favor against the massive Philistine force. After waiting seven days, the men began to scatter, so Saul decided to make the offering himself. Interestingly, Saul's behavior was very similar to Bernie Madoff's. Like Madoff, Saul became fearful when the "market" turned against him. Rather than wait for things to improve (i.e., for God's prophet to arrive), he created a burnt offering that was a fraud.

In any case, Samuel arrived just as Saul finished the offering and said, "What have you done?" Saul's response exposed his growing pride, his fear, and a profound lack of trust in God. Samuel didn't mince words, and he told Saul that what he had done was foolish. He had broken God's command, and Saul's kingdom — that is, through his lineage — would not continue. God would select someone else, a man "after his own heart," to rule the people. In short, Samuel told Saul that the *ascribed* honor of kingship was being taken from his family line due to this significant dishonorable act that resulted in a loss of *acquired* honor. You see, Saul dishonored Samuel, God's prophet, by usurping his role. He also dishonored God with his lack of trust.

In contrast, in the chapter that follows, Saul's son, Jonathan, though grossly outnumbered, trusted in God, mounted a surprise raid on the Philistine camp, and prevailed. His heroism and courage rallied the Israelite troops, and they were able to defeat the Philistines. What is most interesting about how this occurred is the fact that Jonathan did not tell Saul that he was going to mount this sneak attack. Was it because he was aware fear had led his father to violate God's command and perform the unlawful sacrifice? Or was Jonathan starting to find it difficult to honor a father who had behaved dishonorably? Unfortunately, future events would make Jonathan's dilemma much worse.

You see, as Saul came to terms with the fact that he had lost the kingdom, his behavior became more and more reprehensible. For example, below is a list of a few things that Saul did that, if done by any father, would make it difficult, if not impossible, for a child to honor him:

Made unwise decisions and treated others harshly—After Jona-than's surprise attack, the Israelite army chased the Philistines for a day. As you can imagine, at the end of the day, the Israelite army was tired and very hungry. But Saul made a rash vow to God that if anyone ate, they would be put to death. As king, Saul was not leading the chase and probably was getting plenty to eat. Also, remember, Saul had just been told that he was to lose his kingdom. Therefore, it is quite likely Saul was trying to gain favor with God. Perhaps this was another "sacrifice" to try and make up for his disobedience. In any case, Jonathan didn't know about Saul's vow and ate honey to rally his strength. Saul was going to kill Jonathan, but the people rose up against him, so he had to break his vow.

Allowed fear of man to influence him—In 1 Samuel 15, Samuel told Saul to attack the Amalekites and to destroy everyone and all that they had. However, Saul disobeyed God's direct com-mand. He kept the Amalekite king alive and reserved the choice livestock. When Samuel confronted Saul about his disobedience, he initially lied. But when the bleating sheep gave him away, Saul changed his story again and said that he kept the livestock to sac-rifice them to God ... and then they were going to destroy what was left over. But obedience is better than sacrifice. So, of course, Samuel was not swayed by this new story either. Then Saul admit-ted the truth. He feared the people who wanted to keep the spoils and obeyed them rather than God.

Allowed jealousy to consume him—A good definition of jeal-ousy is to spend more time counting someone else's blessings than your own. And, in the case of David, Saul was certainly guilty of this. After David defeated Goliath (1 Sam. 17), the women of Israel celebrated by singing, "Saul has slain his thousands, and

David his tens of thousands" (1 Sam. 18:7). This incensed Saul so much that the next day, he twice tried to kill David with a spear. Saul failed, but his jealousy drove him to waste much of the rest of his life trying to kill David.

Lied to his children and used them in dishonorable ways—Saul was so intent on killing David that he even lied to his children and tried to use them against David. For example, Saul encouraged David to marry his daughter Michal so that she could be used as a "snare" for him (1 Sam. 18:21). Also, he tried to use the close relationship that David and Jonathan shared to set several traps in order to kill David. In fact, when Jonathan challenged Saul about his desire to kill David, asking, "Why should he be put to death? What has he done?" (1 Sam. 20:32), Saul became so enraged that he threw a spear at Jonathan in order to kill him. Not surprisingly, Jonathan was fiercely angry after this incident. Saul's jealousy never led to David's death, but it did alienate him from a son who was called by God to honor him.

As one would imagine, any father who behaved the way that Saul did would make it nearly impossible for his children to honor him. And this certainly was the case regarding Saul and Jonathan. Because of Saul's dishonorable behavior toward God, Samuel, David, and his children, he ended up being disgraced. Like Bernie Madoff, Saul was not able to pass the "family business" on to his offspring. In short, he lost it all. And this should be a "bad dad" lesson for us all to remember.

REFLECTION: THINK ON THESE THINGS

In this chapter, we discussed the difference between ascribed honor, which every dad gets from God, and acquired honor, which is gained or lost based on one's actions. Obviously, acquired honor is something that every dad has the ability to control. So I would like you to take a few moments to reflect on how you are doing in this area. Consider examples of Saul's dishonorable mistakes detailed above. Are you challenged in these areas? If not, how about in other areas related to your behavior with your wife, your children, or the public? Make a list of specific challenges you face.

CORRECTION: CHANGE THESE THINGS

Using the areas that you have listed in the Reflection section, now pick a few of these items and outline the specific actions that you need to do to change your behavior from being dishonorable to honorable. For example, let's say that you have a habit of speaking harshly to your wife, especially in front of your children. This would clearly be a dishonorable act that is hurtful to her and damaging to your children. Accordingly, you may want to meditate on James 3:1 – 12 and other verses which address the taming of the tongue.

CONNECTION: DO THIS THING

Now that you have reflected upon what God needs you to do to make sure your children can obey the fifth commandment and honor you, and you have identified what behavior you need to correct, it's time for you to make the Good Dad Promise. You need to make this promise to God, to yourself, to your wife (or the mother of your children), and to your children.

GOOD DAD

PROMISE #4

I will not make it difficult for my children to honor me.

BAD DAD

MISTAKE #5

CHAPTER SIX

ABRAHAM

HE ABANDONED HIS CHILD

Fathers, do not exasperate your children; instead, bring them up in the training and instruction of the Lord.

Ephesians 6:4

AT FIRST GLANCE, these two men would appear to have nothing in common. One was a white European who had a privileged and international upbringing. He traveled a great deal and was educated at the finest schools. The other man grew up as a poor, black, island boy. Comfort was hard to come by for as long as he could remember. Although he was a smart kid, he only got a chance to attend school sporadically.

Yet these two men—Anders Behring Breivik, Norway's mass murderer, and Lee Boyd Malvo, the "DC Beltway" sniper—though from two very different worlds, are forever connected. They are "brothers." They are fatherless boys who terrorized a nation and killed the innocent.

The terror of the DC sniper shootings is still fresh in my mind. I had just moved to the area to head the National Fatherhood Initiative. The community was paralyzed with fear and rightfully so. You see, the sniper's strategy was to shoot people at random while they were doing normal daily activities. So even mundane tasks like pumping gas became acts of courage.

I also remember well when the news reported that they had caught the alleged shooters, a forty-one-year-old man and a seventeen-year-old boy, and it appeared that the boy had done most of the killing. Instantly, I knew that there was a fatherhood story in this somehow.

And there was.

Quickly, the story began to unfold of how Malvo came under his accomplice John Muhammad's sway.[1,2] Malvo, obedient and eager to please, started calling Muhammad "Dad" soon after they met and even added "John" to his given name in honor of his new "father." The news stories also described how Muhammad, with military precision, trained his new "son" how to kill, Malvo's first victim a twenty-one-year-old mother named Kenya Cook shot in the face at point-blank range.[3]

In October 2012, Malvo, at twenty-seven years old, did an interview with *Today Show* host Matt Lauer that gives significant insight into the sway that Muhammad had on his young life. He offered, "He [Muhammad] knew exactly what motivated me, what I longed for, what was lacking ... I couldn't say 'no.' I had wanted that level of love and acceptance and consistency for all of my life, and couldn't find it."[4]

But there was another story as well. The story of Lee Malvo's real dad, Leslie Malvo, who had four children by as many women, exiting Lee's life when he was six years old. He didn't even know that his teenage son was living in the US. He hadn't spoken to his son in four years and only learned from press reports that his son was the DC sniper. In fact, when reporters found Leslie Malvo in

Jamaica, he could only say that he remembered his son as a "nice kid."[5]

Breivik's childhood story is eerily similar to Malvo's. His parents divorced when he was about one. And, like Malvo, he was described as a "regular Norwegian boy."[6]

But Anders began to change when he was about fifteen. Jens David Breivik, his diplomat father, had remarried and lived in Paris. For a time Anders visited his father, but as he grew into his teen years, his behavior became more rebellious. He started hanging out with a rowdy gang in Oslo, known for tagging graffiti on public buildings. Father and son grew apart, with each one blaming the other for the estrangement. Jens said, "I was always willing to see him, and he knew that. It was Anders who cut it off."[7] But Anders's rambling fifteen-hundred-page "manifesto" reveals his pain and deep-seated resentment toward his father: "I have not spoken to my father since he isolated himself when I was 15 ... He has four children but has cut contact with all of them. So it is pretty clear whose fault that was ... I tried to contact him five years ago but he said that he was not mentally prepared for a reunion."[8]

Like Malvo's father, Jens Breivik was similarly disconnected from his son when reporters found him. He too learned through the media that his son was a mass murderer. Like Malvo's father, Jens had relationships with numerous women. Now racked with shame, Jens said in a TV interview, "In my darkest moments I think that rather than killing all those people he should have taken his own life.... Thinking about what has happened, I get so upset, and I still don't understand that something like this could happen. No normal human being would do something like that."[9]

The journey from boyhood to manhood can be a perilous one.

Boys can become prey for dangerous individuals, as in Malvo's case, or dangerous ideologies, as in Brevik's case. That's why boys need involved and loving fathers to guide them. Indeed, boys have a "hole in their soul" in the shape of their dads. I believe that God whispers into the wombs of their mothers that he has set apart a special man who will love them like no other. But when a father is unable or unwilling to fill that "hole" and fulfill his role, his absence can leave a wound that is not easily healed. And, too often, wounded people wound others.

Lest I be misunderstood, I am in no way making excuses for Malvo and Breivik's behavior. They made evil choices and are responsible for their behavior. There is never a good excuse for killing the innocent. But there is an explanation, one that is so obvious it is often overlooked. You see, we have spent the last forty or so years telling ourselves, and the boys who need them, that fathers don't matter. They are superfluous relics of the past who are not essential to the well-being of their children. Well, the Malvos and Breiviks of the world shout loudly this is just not so. The question is, will we listen, or will we give them more "brothers"?

Now, am I saying a child who is abandoned by a father is destined to become a mass murderer? Of course not. But social science research and anecdotal evidence suggest there is a troubling correlation worth noting. Boys who grow up without their fathers are significantly more likely to have some type of run-in with the criminal justice system. In my work with National Fatherhood Initiative, I have firsthand experience with this unfortunate statistic.

Several years ago, I had an opportunity to visit Louisiana State Penitentiary, also known as "Angola." This notorious prison, which sits on eighteen thousand acres, has the distinction of being the largest maximum-security facility in the country with over

5,200 inmates. Of note, the average sentence in the prison is eighty-eight years, and 3,600 of the 5,200 inmates have a sentence of life without any chance of parole. Also, Angola, which is located at the end of Louisiana Highway 66, is unlike most prisons. It has a cemetery. It is figuratively and literally the end of the road.

I was visiting the prison that day because a group of inmate fathers were running National Fatherhood Initiative's InsideOut Dad® program, which is designed to help incarcerated dads stay connected to their children. Most male inmates are fathers, and most of them grew up without good fathers. And the most poignant predictor of whether children will become incarcerated is if they have a parent who was or is in prison. So the powerful transformation that happens when these fathers go through the InsideOut Dad® program is important because it's key to breaking the intergenerational crime link within families. (There is a Christian version of the InsideOut Dad program that National Fatherhood Initiative developed in partnership with Prison Fellowship that helps inmate fathers come to faith in Christ as well.)

Although I had an opportunity to speak with many fathers that day, there was one dad whose story I will never forget. He was about thirty-five years old, and he told me he was raised without his father. When he was just seventeen, he lost control and got into trouble ... serious trouble. He murdered someone, so he is now serving a life sentence for first-degree murder. Moreover, between the time of the crime and his conviction, he got a young girl pregnant.

But this was not the most troubling aspect of his story.

He told me this was not his first time at Angola prison. It was his second. When he was about seven years old, he came to Angola to meet his father for the first time in his young life. He told me he always swore he would never be like his father. But now he had become him. Now, he had just one goal, and that was to make sure his seventeen-year-old son doesn't continue the family tradition.

As I listened to this father talk about his life behind bars and his past, I could detect in him—like so many incarcerated dads I meet—a deep-seated hurt and woundedness as a result of his father's absence. After all, you are bone of his bone and flesh of his flesh. And a dad is someone who is supposed to love, protect, and guide you like no other. But when a father makes bad choices that result in him being locked up, how does one make sense of this abandonment, especially as a child? Alas, this type of rejection is profound. Is it any wonder that the way some boys assuage their pain is through rage and violence? I think not.

The fact is there is a brewing rage in our midst. We see signs of this in our schools and neighborhoods and in the media that is consumed by young people, especially in their music. For example, recently I was reviewing the lyrics to the song "Cleaning Out My Closet" by Eminem, who is the biggest-selling rap artist of the last decade. In fact, he has sold over eighty million records and earned eleven Grammys. So it is clear the message in his style of music is resonating and connecting with a very diverse audience, especially young men. In this autobiographical song, his rage is palpable when he speaks about his father, who abandoned him when he was just a few months old. He says, "I wonder if he even kissed me goodbye. No, on second thought, I just wish he would ... die."

Not surprisingly, Eminem, who is now an unmarried father, has had a tumultuous life, which has included a recent battle with drug addiction. You see, despite his attempts, I don't believe that he has truly been able to "clean his closet" of the damage that his father's absence left behind. His father left him when he was six months old, and Eminem never knew him. There is still pain there. Note what he said in a recent *60 Minutes* interview with Anderson Cooper, when Cooper asked him if he'd like to meet his father:

> I don't know. I don't know. Some people ask me that. I don't think I do ... if my kids were moved to the edge of the Earth, I'd find them. No doubt in my mind. No money, no nothin', if I had nothing, I'd find my kids. So, there's no excuse. There's no excuse.[10]

Today, about twenty-five million children—one out of three nationally and two out of three in African American families—live in homes apart from their fathers.[11] Certainly, there are a number of reasons why a father may not be in the home, but, sadly, in too many of these cases, the father has simply abandoned his children. When their relationship with the mother ends, so does the relationship with their children. In fact, about 40 percent of the children in father-absent homes see their fathers less than once a month.[12] And many don't see their fathers at all. So this is a very big issue. We have sown the wind and are now reaping a whirlwind of negative consequence because kids in father-absent homes are significantly more at risk for low academic performance, teen pregnancy, behavior problems, and more.[13] And that's why the story of Abraham and his treatment of his son Ishmael is so relevant today. Alas, he made a "bad dad" mistake all dads should avoid.

THE BIRTH OF ISHMAEL

I have been a Christian for many years, and I have heard countless sermons about Abraham and his role as a father. It struck me recently that every sermon focused on Abraham as a father to Isaac. However, Abraham had another son named Ishmael, who was his firstborn. His relationship with Ishmael was very different, and I believe there are some important lessons for all dads to learn by examining this relationship. So let's look at this part of Abraham's life in more detail.

In terms of Abraham as a father, the story really begins in Genesis 15. God came to Abraham in a vision to again affirm the promise that his reward would be great. You see, when God first called Abraham, God told him he would be a great nation (Gen. 12:2). Many years had passed, Abraham was now very old, and he still did not have a child. Yet God made a covenant with Abraham and assured him that his offspring would be as numerous as the stars in the sky.

Time continued to pass, probably more than ten years, and Abraham's wife, Sarah, decided it was time to take things into her own hands. She suggested to Abraham that he sleep with her servant Hagar and produce a child through her. There was an ancient Mesopotamian custom whereby a barren wife could offer her servant to her husband and, if a child were born, he or she would essentially belong to the wife, much like what happens today in a surrogate mother situation. Then the child would be adopted by the father. Sounds like a plan. Right? Well, it did to Abraham, and he slept with Hagar, and she conceived.

But let's pause here for a moment and consider what Abraham knew before he made this decision. First, in Genesis 15, since Abraham was still without a son, he had decided to make Eliezer of Damascus his heir, but God nixed this plan and told Abraham he would give him a son. Second, what Sarah presented to Abraham was a "custom." Nowhere does she say the plan came from God. It was *her* plan. And whenever someone suggests you follow custom and tradition rather than God's plan, you have a clear danger sign that should not be ignored. After all, Abraham talked to God. So prior to making this very important decision, he should have made sure Sarah's plan was God's plan. Finally, Abraham was dealing with a wife who was clearly insecure about her barrenness. In a contemporary sense, Sarah asking Abraham to sleep with Hagar is like a husband being asked by his wife if a dress makes her look fat. Every husband that has been married for more than a day knows he is on dangerous territory in that situation!

In any case, Abraham made the wrong choice, and it started him down the "bad dad" path. Predictably, once Hagar got pregnant, she starting showing contempt for Sarah. When Abraham wouldn't deal with the problem as Sarah requested, she dealt harshly with Hagar, who then fled into the wilderness. An angel of the Lord found Hagar there and told her to return to Sarah. Then the angel told her that she was going to have a son whom she was to name Ishmael. Her son would be a "wild donkey of a man" (Gen. 16:12), and his hand would be against everyone and everyone's hand would be against him. So Hagar did as the angel instructed and gave birth to Ishmael when Abraham was eighty-six years old.

THE BIRTH OF ISAAC

Now the situation is about to get *really* problematic for Abraham.

When Abraham is about a hundred years old, God says to Abraham that he is going to give him a son to be named Isaac ... through Sarah. And God would establish his covenant through Isaac. Certainly, you would expect this to be a time of celebration

101

for Abraham, but interestingly, he said, "If only Ishmael might live under your blessing!" (Gen. 17:18). In other words, he was saying, "Ah … God, I already have a plan in place … It would be much easier if you could just bless it. O Lord, please bless this mess!"

You see, by this time, Ishmael was already about thirteen years old. Abraham had already adopted, circumcised, and bonded with him. Since he was operating from the perspective that Sarah's plan was God's plan, it's safe to assume that Abraham had already told Ishmael he was the child of the covenant. So now he had a real problem.

Soon, just as God promised, Sarah became pregnant and gave birth to Isaac. And Abraham circumcised him after eight days. However, the Bible says that when Isaac was weaned, Abraham had a great feast to honor the occasion, and a big problem arose. Sarah became angry when she saw Ishmael "mocking" Isaac (Gen. 21:9). She demanded that Abraham immediately get rid of that "slave woman" and her son. Abraham didn't want to do so, but God told Abraham to do as Sarah asked. So Abraham gave Hagar and Ishmael some food and water and sent them into the wilderness. In short, he abandoned them. The good news was that God was a faithful Father to the fatherless, saving Ishmael from certain death. However, this does not exempt Abraham from responsibility for a significant "bad dad" event, especially when viewed from Ishmael's perspective.

Bear in mind, Ishmael was the firstborn son who normally would receive his father's blessing and the lion's share of the inheritance. Now all of these things would go to Isaac. Since Abraham had thought Ishmael was the son of the covenant, he assuredly treated him this way, pouring his knowledge and wisdom into him. Now Ishmael was abandoned and near death in the desert, watching his mother die as well. I imagine he must have been wondering what was so wrong with him that his father would reject and abandon him like this. I also suspect a rage was growing inside of him and the seeds were planted that would create a "wild donkey of a man" who would be at war with everyone.

The story of Abraham and Ishmael is an ancient one with contemporary relevance. Frankly, one could easily say Abraham had a "God-ordained" excuse to abandon Ishmael. But to say this is to miss the point. Abraham was the one who sinned by not waiting on God. Ishmael was simply the consequence of Abraham's sin. And, just like today, too often our children must unfairly suffer the consequences of their fathers' sin. For example, consider the children of the incarcerated fathers that I mentioned previously. They are at risk because they lack present fathers to guide and protect them. Or consider the married father who chose to pursue a "soul mate" that was not his wife, and now he no longer can be a father to his children because his ex-wife, so full of hurt and unforgiveness, denies him access to his children. Like Abraham's, these are "bad dad" mistakes that leave children vulnerable, wounded, and more often than we like to admit, enraged.

REFLECTION: THINK ON THESE THINGS

Abraham and Ishmael's story focuses on the effects of physical abandonment. However, I would like to expand the notion of what it means to abandon a child. Consider the words of Chick-fil-A restaurant founder S. Truett Cathy from his book *It's Better to Build Boys Than Mend Men*:

> In a real sense, I had been "fatherless." My father was alive. In fact, he was home every night, and I never knew him to gamble or drink or cheat on my mother. But he never told me, "I love

you." And, when I needed help, like the time when I was sick on a rainy Sunday morning and had to get the newspapers delivered, I knew not to even ask him. As I grew to manhood, my father and I never discussed the difficult issues in life.[14]

Good fathers do three things for their children. They provide, nurture, and guide, which means that they connect to their children physically, emotionally, and spiritually. But it's possible for a father to be physically present but emotionally and spiritually absent from his children's lives. And this kind of absence or abandonment is just as painful for children. So take a few minutes and consider how you are doing as a dad. Would your child say about you what Truett Cathy said about his father? If so, list for yourself a few changes that you need to make.

In this chapter, I said that children have a hole in their soul in the shape of their dads. And when fathers are unwilling or unable to fill that hole, it can leave wounds that are not easily healed. God helped me see that my wound from my own experience of fatherlessness was impacting how I was fathering my children. I have written a short essay called "Holes and Wounded Souls" (Appendix A) to help you understand this issue. I strongly recommend that you read and reflect upon this essay, especially if you grew up without your father. Has a "father wound" affected your fathering? If so, how?

CORRECTION: CHANGE THESE THINGS

If you have abandoned your child — physically, emotionally, spiritually, or all three — figuring out how to make things right can be challenging. After all, it's likely that your child is hurt and/or angry. Plus, your child may have a difficult time putting emotions into words. That's why, as a father, you must be proactive and take the initiative to restore the relationship. I have found that focusing on the 3Rs (Repent, Reconcile, and Restore) works very well in these situations. Consider this analogy that illustrates this point.

Let's say you had an antique chair in your home that had been passed down through your family for generations. In fact, this chair is so precious that no one is allowed to sit in it. Heck, you even have a sign posted near it that reads "Don't Sit in This Chair!" Imagine that I came to your home, willfully or stupidly disregarded the sign, sat on the chair, and broke it. You would be pretty angry, right? Now, what if I started grabbing the pieces to try and put it back together. My sense is that you would be so upset you would tell me to get away from the chair and not touch anything. Why? Because I tried to put the chair back together without saying that I was sorry.

However, if I immediately started apologizing profusely (i.e., repented) for my carelessness and I promised to be more careful in the future, chances are your heart would soften. In other words, my apology would significantly change your attitude and how you viewed the situation. Why? Repentance is a sign of remorse and contrition. Now, if I said that I wanted to make things right by helping to put the chair back together, odds are that you would be more likely to accept my help.

And therein lies a powerful lesson that fathers often forget. Because men are doers and because saying that you're sorry takes true humility, too often, fathers make the mistake of trying to reconcile before they repent. Remember, Proverbs 15:1 says that a soft word turns away wrath. An apology, which reflects true repentance, is the soft word that is needed.

So, after I have repented, we can start putting the chair back together. The word *reconcile* means "to settle or resolve." When you have abandoned your child, you will need to seek forgiveness so that you will be able to settle or resolve the break in your relationship. The "superglue" called commitment is critical in order to bind you heart-to-heart with your child. However, be prepared for a roller coaster of emotions and some difficulties. Most likely, this will not be an easy process. It will take time, but repentance and reconciliation are essential for the well-being of your child.

Now that the pieces have been put back together, it is starting to look like a chair again. But whenever something is broken, there will always be a few pieces that you can't find or just won't fit together like they did originally. So you will need to add some wood putty to fill in these gaps. You will need to sand it to smooth out the rough spots. And you will need to varnish it to make it as much as possible like it was before. The final step is to *restore*, which means to reestablish, recover, or rejuvenate. From a relationship perspective, this means to establish trust, which, once broken, can only be proven by testing and passing the test. After all, the only way to know if a chair has been truly restored is to sit in it!

Finally, it's critical that you bear in mind that you may need to go through the "3R" process with your wife or the child's mother. Remember, Abraham abandoned Ishmael *and* Hagar. So it's safe to assume that Hagar had a fair amount of resentment toward Abraham as well. Mothers are very sensitive to the pain that their children experience. Accordingly, if you are trying to rebuild a relationship with a child who feels abandoned like Ishmael, you will probably have to rebuild a relationship with an abandoned mother who feels like Hagar.

CONNECTION: DO THIS THING

Now that you have reflected upon what God needs you to do to ensure your children do not feel abandoned, and you have identified what you need to correct, it's time for you to make the Good Dad Promise. You need to make this promise to God, to yourself, to your wife (or the mother of your children), and to your children.

GOOD DAD

PROMISE #5

I will not abandon my children.

BAD DAD

MISTAKE #6

CHAPTER SEVEN

ELI

HE FAILED TO DISCIPLINE HIS CHILDREN

Discipline your children, for in that there is hope; do not be a willing party to their death.

Proverbs 19:18

ON JULY 23, 2011, twenty-seven-year-old singer Amy Winehouse was found dead in her home. She had joined the infamous "27 Club"—a proverbial last gig for musicians who died at her age—which includes notable headliners like Jimi Hendrix, Janis Joplin, Jim Morrison, and Kurt Cobain. Although the police reports initially listed the cause of her death as unexplained pending an autopsy, there was little doubt in most people's minds that her demise was the result of years of alcohol and drug abuse. In fact, in 2008, Alex Haines, Winehouse's former personal assistant, publicly expressed his concern about her behavior. He said, "It was my job to look after her. But it was impossible. I thought she wouldn't survive the year with all the drugs and self-harming.... She'd keep taking drugs until she passed out. I reckon she spent £3,500 [$5,000] a week on them."[1]

It is sadly ironic that one of Winehouse's biggest hits was the bluesy song "Rehab," where she declared, "They tried to make me go to rehab, and I said no, no, no." Unfortunately, her life imitated her art — to the bitter end.

Given my interest in fatherhood, there was one line in "Rehab" that I found especially disturbing. It's when Winehouse croons, "I ain't got the time and if my daddy thinks I'm fine ..." Since Winehouse was a prolific songwriter and many of her lyrics were autobiographical, I wondered if her daddy really thought she was fine.

Well, it turns out that he did ... at least initially.

In 2012, Mitch Winehouse released a book titled *Amy, My Daughter*, which recounts the event that inspired "Rehab" and, specifically, this troubling refrain in the song. In the summer of 2004, as Amy was starting to have some success, she began to drink excessively. In fact, on one occasion, she became so drunk that she fell, hit her head, and had to go to the hospital. After she was released from the hospital, one of her best friends and her managers met with Mitch Winehouse to discuss what they referred to as "Amy's drinking problem."[2] They wanted Amy to go to rehab immediately, but her father had other ideas. He wrote: "I was against it. I thought she'd just had one too many this time, and rehab seemed an overreaction. 'I think she's fine,' I told everyone, which later turned into a line in 'Rehab.'"[3]

After more persuasion, Mitch was convinced to support the plan to get Amy to go to rehab. But it's telling that instead of taking his daughter to the facility, he left this task to her managers. Not surprisingly, Amy didn't stay long, returning home in just a few hours. Despite her managers' attempts to persuade her to return, she refused. Apparently, the rehab clinic felt that her condition required at least a two months' stay. However, Amy stated, "I haven't got the time...,"[4] and she would deal with this situation in her own way. Clearly, her father took her side. He wrote: "Initially, I agreed with her, since I hadn't been totally convinced she needed to go in the first place."[5]

As the years passed and her fame grew, it did became apparent to her father that Amy needed serious help. In fact, in 2008, her father resolved to help his daughter get clean from what was now not only an alcohol problem, but also a heroin and crack cocaine addiction as well. Her father desperately tried to get or to keep his daughter in rehab and off drugs. But too often she said, "No, no, no ..." She would not listen to his advice or heed his warnings. Although she would eventually make some progress getting off drugs, she continued to struggle with alcohol for the rest of her short life.

A STRONG-WILLED CHILD AND AN OVERINDULGENT DAD

As you read Mitch Winehouse's story, it's very clear that he deeply loved his daughter, and she loved him too. She even had a large "Daddy's Girl" tattoo on her left arm. As a father who has sons about the age of Amy Winehouse at her death, my heart truly goes out to him. That said, it's also clear that he was unable to help his daughter discipline herself to resist the destructive temptations that ultimately killed her. Clearly, no one loves a child more than a parent, so why at the first sign of trouble didn't he push as hard as her managers to get her into rehab? Why did he give in, letting Amy have her way?

As I read his book, it struck me that the seeds for Mitch Winehouse's behavior may have been planted in Amy's early childhood.

As his narrative revealed more about Amy's temperament and character, it's clear that his daughter was a classic strong-willed child. He paints a picture of a young girl determined to *always* have her own way. And it seems, even at a young age, at critical points she got it. For example, when Amy was just twelve, she wanted to attend drama school full-time, but her parents were against it. So, without telling them, she applied to the Sylvia Young Theatre School. I was surprised to read that when she was accepted, her parents let her attend. No doubt, a parent allowing a child, no matter how talented, to get his or her way after being disobedient and dishonest in this way would send the wrong message, especially to a strong-willed child.

Sadly, this same pattern of behavior emerged later in her life—with dire consequences. In 2005, she met a guy named Blake Fielder-Civil and fell madly in love with him. But there was a big problem. Blake was a heroin and cocaine addict. Given Amy's problem with drinking, her father was concerned that Blake's drug habit would become her habit too. Predictably, it did. He was also concerned that Amy would marry Blake without him knowing, and he made her promise that she would tell him about any wedding plans beforehand. However, without telling him or her mother, she married Blake on a trip to Miami. She did it "her way." Unfortunately, one of Blake's primary tasks as her husband was to facilitate Amy's drug habit, and according to Mitch Winehouse, Blake even brought Amy drugs while she was in rehab.

Finally, Mitch Winehouse describes his daughter as "mischievous, bold, and daring"[6] and recounts stories about Amy being a risk-taker as a young girl, at times not listening to him or others, even when it was in her best interest to do so. In every school that she attended, she was "disruptive and attention-seeking,"[7] and

116

he and Amy's mother received regular complaints about Amy's behavior. In short, she had a consistent record of disciplinary problems that were sure to impact her later in life.

Why? Because Amy Winehouse had chosen a profession that required a tremendous amount of personal discipline, impulse- and self-control, which her history suggests were things that she struggled with all of her life. The entertainment business can be a dangerous place, and folks in the business don't often warn you of its pitfalls. Rather, they are happy to turn your funeral into an excuse for another party. Plus, as notables like Elvis Presley and Michael Jackson prove, you may be worth more dead than alive. You see, Amy Winehouse wanted to be very famous. She made this clear in her secret application to the Sylvia Young Theatre School. But fame can be intoxicating, and history is replete with sad stories of entertainers who had one drink of fame too many and lost their way.

That said, in his book, Mitch Winehouse gives several important clues which illustrate clearly why he struggled to truly discipline his daughter when she was young. First, when Amy was about ten years old, he left her mother, whom he describes as a good wife and mother, for another woman. Now, of course, this act would not necessarily lead a child down a path of drug and alcohol addiction. But it can lead a father down a problematic path in terms of his ability to appropriately discipline his children. And it appears that this is exactly what may have happened to Mitch Winehouse. By his own admission, due to his guilt over leaving Amy's mother, he began to overindulge his children. He writes of Amy: "She was wild, but I indulged her; I couldn't help myself. I know I over-compensated my children for the divorce."[8]

He also shares that he would buy presents for no reason, take his kids to expensive places, and give them money, as a result of his guilt. In my years of working with fathers, I have seen similar behavior, especially when a father has caused the breakup of his family. A father can fall into the trap of trying to replace his presence with "presents"—and become a "Disneyland" dad who loses his way in the important area of discipline because he desperately wants his children to love and forgive him. Interestingly, a father's moral failings and lack of personal discipline can cause him to believe he has lost his moral standing with his children and, thereby, the authority to discipline them.

Moreover, it's quite revealing that Mitch Winehouse says that he essentially overindulged his children. To overindulge is to indulge in something excessively, especially to drink immoderately or to binge. So if you overindulge someone, you are yielding excessively to his or her wishes. In other words, a father who overindulges his children is not disciplining them, but actually doing and modeling the opposite. Therefore, it is not surprising that his children, especially the strong-willed ones, would have a difficult time resisting temptation and exhibiting self-control, even when it was in their best interest to do so.

Second, Mitch Winehouse's fathering was further complicated by the fact he was enamored with his daughter's precocious talent. When she was a little girl, he would have her perform for him and her mother. He was grooming her to be an entertainer, which was also a dream he had for himself. Of note, after his daughter's death, he recorded his first album, titled *Rush of Love*. On his website he says: "Well of course I wouldn't be in this position without Amy ... but now the opportunity is there, why not take it? Who wouldn't want to make an album?"[9]

He and Amy had a very special connection through music that

remained even after he left the family home. Indeed, their "love language" was lyrical. Moreover, he helped shape his daughter's musical taste and the distinctive sound, modeled after jazz greats like Ella Fitzgerald, Sarah Vaughan, and Billie Holliday, which would bring her (and him) fame and wealth.

Of course, there is nothing inherently wrong with a father nurturing and helping develop his child's talent. But there is a danger that a father must be attentive to. He can't get so vested in his child's success that he loses his ability to discipline her. You see, especially with a father who is prone to overindulge, if his child's success becomes his identity, and if his child's fame becomes his fame, it's easier for him to say "she's fine," even when she is not.

DISCIPLINE IS LOVE

The story of Mitch and Amy Winehouse serves as a poignant reminder that one of the most important tasks that God gives fathers is to discipline their children. In fact, you don't have to read very much of the Bible before you find verses that reflect this point. For example, Proverbs 23:13 warns us not to withhold discipline from our children. Proverbs 13:24 goes even further because it says that if we love our children, we will be careful to discipline them. And I am sure you have heard often that we should make sure that we discipline our children in love. But this verse in Proverbs makes a more direct statement that discipline *is* love and if we don't do it, we actually hate our children. Powerful stuff indeed!

This notion of discipline as love really started to make more sense to me many years ago when my older son was about to graduate from the eighth grade. As part of our church's graduation ceremony, each father was asked to say a few words about his child, something that you felt God had shown you regarding your child's transition from grade school to high school.

This was an interesting assignment for me because my son was moving quickly through puberty. He was becoming a man, and I was becoming increasingly aware that the day was fast approaching when he would no longer be in my home. As I considered just how soon that day would arrive, I remembered Psalm 127:3–5, which reads:

> Children are a heritage from the LORD,
>   offspring a reward from him.
> Like arrows in the hands of a warrior
>   are children born in one's youth.
> Blessed is the man
>   whose quiver is full of them.

Most of the time when I have heard fathers mention this verse, it was either in celebration of having a "full quiver" or in celebration of the quiver-filling process. But God brought this verse to mind on this occasion for a very different reason. He wanted to draw my attention to the arrows (i.e., children) and role of the warrior (i.e., the father).

Initially, I found it a bit odd that the Psalmist chose to refer to children as arrows, especially since arrows are often used as a weapon to inflict deadly harm. But as I thought about it more, I came to understand that this was a very appropriate analogy. Yes, arrows have a sharp and dangerous tip. However, an arrow's real danger lies in the seemingly innocuous feathers at the end because they control distance, direction, and flight.

While children are in their father's care, God has tasked him, like a skilled warrior, to diligently trim, prune, and position the "feathers" of his children's character so that when they are launched into the world, they won't miss their God-ordained "mark" and do great harm to themselves and others. This is what discipline is all about. It is a delicate and, at times, unpleasant process, but it is much needed. After all, the only thing more dangerous than an inaccurate warrior is an "undisciplined" arrow. Unfortunately, all you have to do is turn on your local TV news and you will hear countless stories about kids who have caused tremendous physical, emotional, and spiritual damage to themselves and others because no one took the time to "discipline" their feathers. Indeed, one of the saddest "bad dad" stories in the Bible is about a father whose sons sorely missed their mark because he refused to discipline them. It is the story of Eli.

DISCIPLINE IS DESTINY

Now, Eli was clearly a special man to God, so much so that he was not only a high priest but also a judge for the people of Israel for forty years. It's worth noting that there is no record of anyone else having both of these roles at the same time. Therefore, God vested Eli not only with moral authority over the people of Israel, but also with civil authority. Furthermore, it is worth noting that Eli's lineage was a distinguished one, for he was a descendant of a priest named Ithamar, who was Aaron's youngest son.

Given Eli's roles and position, he certainly was well aware of the importance of discipline, especially for one's children, and the importance of respecting the things of God. No doubt, he knew well the Ten Commandments as well as Deuteronomy 6:7, which instructs parents to impress them on their children.

Despite all that he knew and the moral and civil authority God gave him, Eli failed to exercise his authority in the primary place that God gives every father: his own home. And as a result, he raised two sons, Hophni and Phinehas, who became priests like their father. But both grew up to become men that the Bible describes as "scoundrels" (1 Sam. 2:12). They disgraced and dishonored Eli. More importantly, however, they disobeyed God's standards, and their actions led to God's judgment. In fact, God took the lives of all three—Eli, Hophni, and Phinehas—on the same day, removing Eli's family from the priesthood.

The Bible doesn't say anything about Eli's sons when they were little boys, and I have no doubt that Eli loved his sons and desired them to grow up to be godly men. But discipline, not just desire, determines a child's destiny. Unfortunately, Eli failed to trim the feathers of his sons' character, and his failure led to their destruction. Although he tried to rebuke them when he was old (1 Sam. 2:22–25), by that time the damage was already done. And clearly God held Eli accountable, asking him, "Why do you scorn my sacrifice and offering that I prescribed for my dwelling? Why do you honor your sons more than me?" (v. 29).

It would be easy to look at Eli's situation and dismiss it as just another Bible story, but I believe that Eli's challenge and choices as a father are ones that all dads still face today. For some reason, Eli, despite being a father who clearly loved God, was unable to raise sons with godly character. Maybe maintaining two demanding roles as a high priest and as a judge took him away from home during critical points in his sons' life, like today's dads who are challenged to balance work and family. Maybe he overindulged them to make up for his absence. It could also have been that, like too many fathers today, he outsourced his God-ordained role of disciplining his sons to others—to their mom, or to the other religious leaders. We will never really know.

But I believe that there was another dynamic at play here as well. Eli was a descendant of a God-ordained priestly lineage, and no doubt he wanted to see his sons continue in this prestigious role. In a sense, the priesthood was a God-given "talent" his sons possessed, much like Amy Winehouse's unique voice. But to have a long and successful "career" as a priest, you must have more than talent, especially when God is the audience. You must have godly character and discipline. Although the Bible doesn't give specific details in this area, surely Eli had trained his sons how to perform in the role of a priest and how to properly handle the sacrifices. Moreover, since character and discipline problems in adulthood are often evident in childhood, Eli may have seen clear evidence and warning signs that his sons should not have become priests. He may have seen that his sons had a cavalier attitude toward the things of God. But their future was linked to his future.

Also, it's not hard to imagine that soon after Eli turned this sacred trust over to his sons, others knew that his sons were not handling their responsibilities properly. After all, these sacrifices were to atone for all of the people's sins, so the entire community had a vested interest in making sure that they were done properly. Maybe, as in the Amy Winehouse situations, some of the temple workers went to meet with Eli to discuss his sons' "sacrificing problem." They wanted his sons to go to "rehab" to break their immoral habits, but Hophni and Phinehas said, "No, no, no...." Could it be that Eli too said, "They're fine," at least initially? After all, it is difficult to step in when your legacy and identity are vested in your children's success.

Interestingly, much like in the Amy Winehouse situation, there was a proverbial "27 Club" for priests who failed to follow God's regulations that Eli and his sons most assuredly would have known about. Leviticus 10:1–3 tells the story of two of Aaron's sons, Nadab and Abihu, who were consumed instantly by fire after they offered "unauthorized fire" before the Lord. After this happened, Moses was very clear with Aaron and his remaining sons, Eleazar and Ithamar, that if the priest did not honor God's holiness and follow his commands, they would face the penalty of death. The bottom line is that God takes discipline very seriously, and as fathers, we must as well.

You see, every father must daily choose between courage and comfort when it comes to disciplining his children. The problem is that to be comfortable is never courageous and to be courageous is never comfortable. That's why La-Z-Boy chairs aren't airdropped across the enemy lines before the Marines parachute in!

In Eli's case, at least initially, he clearly chose comfort. And maybe this was a pattern that he had used with his sons for many years. After a long day of dealing with the moral and civil issues of the people of Israel, he may have had little energy or interest in dealing with the character problems of his sons. (Sound familiar?)

But the situation didn't get any easier for Eli, because when you don't deal with children's discipline issues early in their lives, it is more difficult to get their attention later in life. Proverbs 22:6 is as much a principle as it is a promise when is says to train children in the way they should go, and when they are old, they will not depart from it. So, if by his action or inaction, a father enables his children to be undisciplined and uncontrolled, odds are that they will not depart from this behavior when they are older.

In any case, I suspect that Eli knew this well. As an old man, he was totally dependent on his scoundrel sons to provide for his physical needs. So he shared in their sin by eating food that was not sacrificed according to God's commandments. It would have taken considerable courage for him to really stand up to his sons because they could have stopped taking care of him. After all, they were his "social security," and he, better than anyone, knew their character. But he also knew God's character, and that his sons' behavior would bring God's judgment, just as Mitch Winehouse knew that his daughter's drug and alcohol use would have dire consequences and could take her life if she didn't stop.

Ironically, if Eli had chosen to be courageous and discipline his sons while they were young, he would have been able to rest in the comfort of their godly character when he was old. Instead, because of his "bad dad" mistake, Eli missed the mark on discipline and, as a result, missed the blessing of sons who would carry on a godly legacy.

REFLECTION: THINK ON THESE THINGS

The word *discipline* comes from the Latin words *disciplina*, which means "teaching" and "learning," and *discipulus*, which means "pupil." Jesus' followers were called *disciples* because they were his pupils, and he was teaching and modeling the way that they should live and treat each other. In the same way, a good father is to be like Jesus for his children. Through his consistent and loving discipline, he must make disciples of his children. He should be a living expression of the apostle Paul's words: "Follow my example, as I follow the example of Christ" (1 Cor. 11:1).

So are you making disciples of your children by the way that you are disciplining them? Or are you missing the mark and need guidance? If so, reflect on these verses:

> Whoever heeds discipline shows the way to life, but whoever
> ignores correction leads others astray. (Prov. 10:17)
> Discipline your children, for in that there is hope; do not be
> a willing party to their death. (Prov. 19:18)

> No discipline seems pleasant at the time, but painful. Later
> on, however, it produces a harvest of righteousness and
> peace for those who have been trained by it. (Heb. 12:11)

CORRECTION: CHANGE THESE THINGS

Ephesians 6:4 warns fathers not to exasperate their children but instead bring them up in the training and instruction of the Lord. When you consider this warning in conjunction with the Psalm 127 reference to children as arrows, it really makes a lot of sense. You see, when we exasperate our children, it's like grinding down the tip of an arrow, creating heat and friction and ultimately rendering the arrow useless. Or it's like breaking the shaft of an arrow so that it is no longer able to fly. Since God designed children to leave a father's quiver and soar to their God-ordained purpose and mark, when fathers exasperate their children, they tend to behave in one of two ways. Either they will retreat from their fathers, or they will rebel against them. In fact, it could have been that Eli so exasperated his sons when they were young that they just started to tune him out and rebel against his instruction, even against their best interests. As Josh McDowell famously says, "Rules without relationship yield rebellion."[10]

Are there things that you need to change when it comes to discipline? Are you exasperating your children by being too harsh or by being inconsistent in your discipline? What are three changes that you need to make so that you don't cause your children to miss the mark?

CONNECTION: DO THIS THING

Now that you have reflected upon what God needs you to do in the area of discipline and you have identified what you need to correct, it's time for you to make the Good Dad Promise. You need to make this promise to God, to yourself, to your wife (or the mother of your children), and to your children.

GOOD DAD

PROMISE #6

I won't miss the mark by failing to
lovingly discipline my children.

BAD
DAD

MISTAKE #7

CHAPTER EIGHT

MANOAH

HE FAILED TO TAME
HIS CHILD'S TALENTS

Train up a child in the way he should go: and when he is old, he will not depart from it.

Proverbs 22:6 (KJV)

WHEN I WAS A KID, I loved reading comic books. I could spend countless hours in my room with a stack of them. One of my favorite comic series was the X-Men. Legendary comics writer Stan Lee and artist Jack Kirby created these characters in the early 1960s, and they remain very popular today. I am not surprised that kids still love this series. After all, the X-Men were a cast of unique mutants born with a special "X-gene," which gave them superhuman powers and talents. Interestingly, these mutants usually discovered their powers early in life, often as children.

But there was a big problem. The mutant's talent could be used either to benefit society or to destroy humanity. In fact, sometimes a mutant's power could pose a danger even to himself or herself. The fortunate ones ended up under the care and training of Professor Xavier, who founded the "Xavier School for Gifted Youngsters." At the school, he would teach mutants how to control and master their considerable powers. However, Professor Xavier could not rescue all of the mutants, so some fell into the clutches of Magneto, Professor Xavier's long-time nemesis, who formed the sinister "Brotherhood of Evil Mutants." Magneto wanted to control the world, and he sought to turn as many mutants as possible to the dark side.

The epic struggle between Professor Xavier and Magneto is an interesting metaphor for the challenges that good fathers face while raising their children. You see, Professor Xavier behaved as a good "father figure" for the mutants in his care. He risked everything, including his own life, to make sure that mutants used their talents for good. On the other hand, Magneto represented the kind of tempter that every father hopes will never have sway over his children, the type of person who seeks to seduce one's kids to use their God-given talents to selfishly benefit themselves or, worse, do harm to others.

Consider the character named "Rogue." A troubled and rebellious teenage runaway, she had the unique talent of being able to absorb the memories, skills, and powers of others simply through skin-to-skin contact. In fact, the longer she maintained contact with someone, the more she would absorb. Moreover, if she touched someone for too long, she would absorb these things permanently. Clearly, Rogue's talent was a double-edged sword that, if untamed, could cause great harm to others. Therefore, it's not surprising that she felt like an outcast for much of her life. Fortunately, Professor Xavier was able to get Rogue to his school, and he helped her master her talent so that it could be used for good.

TALENTED BUT TROUBLED

Recently, I had a thought-provoking conversation with a father who shared that his young son was extremely talented and blessed with some impressive natural abilities. An excellent student and a superb athlete, everything seemed to come easily for him, even making friends. Moreover, he was quick-witted and exceptionally gifted verbally. He was the kind of kid who could "sell ice cubes to an Eskimo."

However, there was one thing that greatly troubled this father. His son was manipulating and extremely disrespectful to him and his wife, often speaking to them rudely and frequently cursing at them. He also treated his younger siblings harshly, physically and verbally, especially when he was trying to impress his friends. To make matters worse, the father's impressionable toddler son was starting to mimic some of the most troubling aspects of his older brother's behavior. This father admitted he had not taken the right steps early on to "nip this problem in the bud," and that he and his wife had indulged and spoiled their firstborn. Now, unfortunately, his entire home was in chaos.

As I listened to the details, like a typical guy, my mind raced quickly to a solution to solve this father's problem. This was an easy one. He simply needed to put his foot down. Immediately starting to set and reinforce boundaries and standards with his firstborn was essential, because his son would soon be a teenager. So that's just what I told him.

He agreed with my assessment wholeheartedly, but as we started to discuss the specifics regarding the changes that he needed to make, I sensed that he was hesitant to take aggressive action. And that's when I figured out that the situation was a bit more complicated than it appeared. Although he was frustrated and concerned about his son's disturbing behavior, it was clear he was conflicted. Despite, and maybe because of, his son's bad behavior, he was popular and considered to be a leader that his friends, and even his siblings, wanted to follow. Wouldn't "taming" his son's considerable talents—even though they were being used in destructive ways—ruin his son's chance at success later in life?

I think that most dads can definitely relate to this father's dilemma. As men, we are wired to compete and achieve. Also, as "proud papas," we often count our children's success as our success. And it's very tempting to say proudly, "That's my boy" when he uses his talents well, even in situations where he hurts others. For dads, the notion of taming a child's talents can be challenging and even seem a bit counterproductive. After all, isn't one of a dad's primary responsibilities to help his children get the most out of their talents?

TALENTS AND THE IMPORTANCE OF CHARACTER

The Bible certainly supports the concept of being a good steward of what God has given us. For example, Jesus made this point very effectively in one of his best-known teachings, "The Parable of the Talents" (Matt. 25:14–30). In the parable, a master (who represents God, our heavenly Father) is going on a journey, and he selects three of his servants and entrusts some money to them. To one servant, he gives five talents of money, to another he gives two talents, and to another, he gives one talent. He then leaves on his trip. The servants who received five and two talents immediately put their money to work and quickly double the amount. But the servant who received one talent simply digs a hole in the ground and hides his master's money.

Well, eventually the master returns, and calls the servants to give an account for what they have done with the money he gave them. Not surprisingly, he is very pleased with the two servants who put their talents to work. But he is extremely upset with the servant who didn't use his talent. So much so, that he even takes the one talent away from him and casts him out into the darkness.

Given our culture's focus on the importance of financial gain, any dad reading this parable could conclude that Jesus' primary objective is to communicate the importance of not wasting your God-given talents, financial or otherwise. Clearly, this is one of the lessons of this passage, and it's easy to see why it would resonate with fathers.

But as I began to reflect more on this passage, it occurred to me that Jesus' parable was less about the amount of talent one received than it was about the *character* of the one who received it. For example, the master was equally pleased with the servants who doubled what they received even though one had been given more than the other. They had unequal talents, but they exhibited equally good character. These two servants used their talents wisely and appropriately, not because of what they expected to gain, but because they wanted to honor and please the master who graciously trusted them with *his* talents. Their character reflected a humility that comes from knowing that all talent is a gift from God and therefore should be maximized for his glory.

Clearly, the servant who buried his one talent had a deeper problem than the fact that he did not double his master's money. (Remember, the master was already rich, and he let the other two servants keep their initial talents and their gain.) This servant's behavior reflected a deep character problem — fear, laziness, or disrespect — that so displeased his master that he was cast outside.

The bottom line is that God, our heavenly Father, places a high value on the character of his children, and therefore so should every earthly father. Let's face it. Every day the news is filled with stories of very talented people who have hurt others and whose lives are in shambles because they never developed godly character and never learned how to tame their talents. In God's economy, a man who has tremendous talents but has poor and ungodly character is little different from a man who has very little talent and ungodly character. Both men miss the mark and won't accomplish their God-ordained purpose in life. That's why a primary responsibility of every father is to tame his children's talents by helping them to develop godly character. Failure to do so can lead to devastating and dire consequences, as we will see in the story of Manoah, the father of Samson.

A VERY SPECIAL SON

One of the examples best known and most often cited of someone whose character hindered him from using his God-given talent appropriately is Samson.

Many books, commentaries, and countless sermons have examined his tragic story. Even Hollywood got into the act, first with the 1949 epic Cecil B. DeMille film and, most recently, with a 1996 TV adaptation starring the beautiful Elizabeth Hurley as the temptress Delilah. These films, like most sermons, tend to focus on Samson and his weakness for the fairer sex. But I think it's important to examine an aspect of the story that few seem to discuss: the role of Samson's father Manoah. First, let's set the scene.

Samson's birth is recorded in Judges 13. He is born during a difficult time for the Israelite people. Because they had done evil in the eyes of the Lord, God allowed them to be delivered into the hands of their dreaded nemesis, the Philistines, for forty years. Accordingly, they are desperate for someone to lead and deliver them.

The Bible says that Manoah's wife was sterile and childless. Then one day an angel of the Lord appeared to her and told her that she was going to have a very special son. The angel told her to avoid anything that was unclean and to shun wine and other fermented drinks. Moreover, she was told that no razor was to ever touch her son's head. Her son would begin the deliverance of Israel from the hands of the Philistines.

As you can imagine, she was very excited and rushed to tell her husband the news. Interestingly, Manoah, a godly man, immediately understood the significance of what his wife told him. So he prayed to the Lord and asked for the angel to come back and teach him how the boy should be raised. When the angel returned, Manoah asked a question that every father should ask of God, "What is to be the rule that governs the boy's life and work?" (Judg. 13:12). You see, Manoah knew that his son was going to have a unique calling and purpose. His son was to be a Nazirite.

Let's pause for a moment and consider the significance of what it means to be a Nazirite. First, usually someone would *choose* to take the vow to become Nazirite. In fact, in Numbers 6:2–21, God tells Moses specifically what to do if someone made this choice. But in this unusual case, God chose Samson before his birth for this vow. God set him apart. His Nazirite vow was a unique and special God-given gift, or even a talent. That's why Manoah wanted the angel to come back. He was confused because he probably had never known of someone being born a Nazirite.

Second, when someone would choose to be a Nazirite, they had the liberty to choose the duration of the vow. In its ordinary form, however, the Nazirite's vow lasted only thirty, and at most one hundred, days.[1] Clearly, Samson's case was very different since he was chosen to take this vow while in his mother's womb.

Again, this must have confused Manoah, but it also signaled to him that he would be raising a very special child with a very special purpose—the deliverance of Israel. This understanding was confirmed because as Samson grew, the Lord blessed him, and the Spirit began to stir in him at an early age.

The Bible doesn't say any more about Samson's childhood. However, given Manoah's concern about how to raise him properly, it's pretty safe to assume that he often told Samson about his unique situation. In fact, I am sure that Manoah and Samson had more than a few conversations about the hair! Plus, the Bible says that the "Spirit of the LORD began to stir" in Samson at an early age (Judg. 13:25). Generally when you find this said about someone in the Old Testament, God is preparing that person to do a mighty work for God's people. (See 1 Sam. 16:13 regarding David and Judg. 3:10 regarding Othneil as examples.) So, from the words of his earthly father and from the Spirit of his heavenly Father, Samson received confirmation throughout his young life that he was something special.

ACCOMMODATE AND PARTICIPATE

However, it becomes quite apparent early in Samson's life that he has a worldly vice that is as much a part of him as his God-given virtue. In Judges 14, the Bible continues with Samson's story. He is now a young man and has just visited Timnah, which was a town in the Philistine territory. Judges 14:2–3 says,

> When he returned, he said to his father and mother, "I have seen a Philistine woman in Timnah; now get her for me as my wife."
>
> His father and mother replied, "Isn't there an acceptable woman among your relatives or among all our people? Must you go to the uncircumcised Philistines to get a wife?"

But Samson said to his father, "Get her for me. She's the right one for me."

Now put yourself in Manoah's place. You have a very gifted and talented son that you know God has set apart for a very specific purpose, but he wants to do something that you clearly know is wrong. After all, Samson was supposed to defeat the Philistines, not marry into them! Much like the father with the talented son that I mentioned above, Manoah was at a critical crossroad, and it was important for the sake of his son that he do the right thing. But, unfortunately, Manoah did not make the right choice. In fact, he made two "bad dad" mistakes, which are listed below, that would help send Samson down the road of untamed sensuality and debauchery.

Accommodate: Although Manoah knew that what Samson was doing deliberately contradicted God's plan for his life, nonetheless, he accommodated his son and submitted to Samson's will. He got Samson the Philistine wife that he wanted but should not have. By doing this, he supported his son's most dangerous vice and most debilitating weakness.

Participate: Judges 14:10 tells us that Manoah participated in Samson's wedding even though there were clear signs that this wedding was a mistake. For example, the bride's family rejected a conventional wedding where the bride becomes part of her husband's family. Instead, Samson's wife would remain with her own people and her children would be considered part of her family.[2] This meant that the Philistines would have considerable leverage over Samson that could hinder him from delivering Israel. In fact, the Philistines exercised this new power over Samson quickly when they got his wife to share with them the answer to his riddle. (See Judg. 14:17.)

Samson's ultimately tragic end is well known. However, Samson's failure to achieve his God-given potential is the most troubling. As a judge for twenty years, gifted from God with the talent to deliver the Israelites from the oppressive Philistine rule, he failed to do so. In fact, most of the time Samson used his talent and power for his own purposes, not for God's or the Israelites'. Even at his death, when he toppled the pillars of the Philistine temple, he was motivated more by revenge than repentance (Judg. 16:28). He was untamed and self-focused to the very end.

And this leads us back to Manoah. Could it be that even as a small boy, Samson was self-focused, impulsive, and motivated by the lust of his eyes? Were there occasions when Samson was a boy that Manoah could have used as "teachable moments," but Manoah chose to accommodate and participate instead? We will never know. But what we do know is that Manoah's behavior and Samson's end are sobering lessons for all dads. If we truly want our children to have and do God's best, we must tame their talents.

REFLECTION: THINK ON THESE THINGS

One of the risks of using Samson's example when thinking about taming a child's talents is to assume that the lessons apply only to a dad who is raising the next NFL star like Tim Tebow or Olympic champion like Gabby Douglas. After all, what's to worry about if you are raising a *normal* kid?

Though I can certainly understand this perspective, I want to challenge you and encourage you to think more broadly and consider talent from God's perspective. Psalm 139:14 says that a child is fearfully and wonderfully made and that God's works are wonderful. What this means is that *every* child is talented in a special God-given way. And God has placed every child on this earth with a purpose that he would like him or her to fulfill. Therefore, God requires every good dad to be in the talent-taming business!

Please spend some moments reflecting on a few of the unique talents of your child or children. I encourage you not to only think about talents in terms of "smarts and sports." There are many different types of talents. Can your daughter make even the saddest person smile? If so, that's a talent. List it. Can your son make all the neighborhood kids follow him? If so, that's a talent. List it. You get the idea.

CORRECTION: CHANGE THESE THINGS

When Manoah was at a crossroad about how to respond when Samson was clearly straying from God's will and call, he made two "bad dad" mistakes. He accommodated, and he participated. Now that you have identified your child or children's talents, have you been making the same mistake that Manoah did? If so, you need to correct this. What are three specific actions that you will take?

Remember, God doesn't want a dad to accommodate a child's behavior that is outside his will. He wants a dad to *transform* it into godly behavior by pointing a child back to his Word and his principles. Nor does God want a dad to participate with a child who is outside of his will. He requires a dad to *guide* his child. This means that a good dad, just like a good shepherd, will lovingly lead his child in the way that he or she should go.

So whenever you are tempted to accommodate, choose to transform; and whenever you are tempted to participate, choose to guide.

CONNECTION: DO THIS THING

Now that you have reflected upon what God needs you to do to make sure that you will tame your child's talents, and you have identified what you need to correct, it's time for you to make the Good Dad Promise. You need to make this promise to God, to yourself, to your wife (or the mother of your children), and to your children.

GOOD DAD

PROMISE #7

I will tame my child's talents.

BAD DAD

MISTAKE #8

CHAPTER NINE

LOT

HE PITCHED HIS FAMILY'S TENT NEAR TEMPTATION

"Watch and pray that you will not fall into temptation. The spirit is willing, but the flesh is weak."

Mark 14:38

SINCE I HAVE BEEN VERY INVOLVED as a national speaker on fatherhood, I usually get a copy of most fatherhood books. Although it is a pleasure to receive all of these books, I particularly enjoy getting the coffee-table-type photography books which feature dads and their children. There are an abundance of negative portrayals of fathers in the media, so it's a treat to see the good guys get the recognition that they rightly deserve. Their stories are typically very compelling, and these books usually feature everyday dads, who, in many cases, have overcome considerable obstacles to be the kind of fathers that their kids need them to be. For example, I recently received a new book called *Choosing Fatherhood: America's Second Chance*. Noted photographer Lewis Kostiner took absolutely wonderful pictures of dads and their children from all walks of life. The book also features compelling and thought-provoking essays about the critical state of father-hood in America.

However, several months ago, I was flipping through one of these photography books featuring good celebrity dads and their children, and I came across a pictorial spread that literally stopped me mid-flip. It was a picture of *Playboy* magazine founder Hugh Hefner and his two sons. The photograph included a touching saccharin-sweet caption that would lead one to believe Hefner is the kind of dad that we all should aspire to be.[1]

Now, I have no desire to try and set myself up as the captain of the dad universe and final arbiter on all things fatherhood, nor do I want to pass judgment on Hefner's right to offspring. After all, as he knows well, it's a free country. However, when I think about good dads, Hugh Hefner just does *not* come to mind. You see, we should celebrate what we want more of. That's why we have birthday parties and wedding receptions. But do we really want more fathers like him? Think about it. Is Hefner really a good role model for his sons (and yours) regarding how they should treat women? And what good dad would want his young daughter to go to the Playboy Mansion for a playdate?

In my view, one of the key responsibilities of any good dad is to help their fellow fathers be good dads as well. And Hef-ner absolutely fails this important test. In fact, he has made his substantial wealth doing the exact opposite. For decades, he has been on a mission to turn good fathers into "peeping daddies." In his role as the godfather of pornography, he has helped destroy countless fathers and families, because pornography is a silent and secret family killer, eye candy that leads to physical, emotional, and spiritual decay. And Hefner prides himself on being the chief candy man. When the Lord's Prayer says "lead me not into temptation," Hugh Hefner comes to mind. But, unfortunately, Hefner has been very successful in spreading his perilous product and worldview.

THE ENTICEMENT OF PORNOGRAPHY

A few summers ago, my neighborhood was infested with Japanese beetles. These ravenous little insects were everywhere. However, since my wife is an avid and dedicated gardener with the most beautiful assortment of plants and bushes on the block, they made our home their home. We tried many tactics to get rid of these creatures but nothing worked. After they devoured the leaves of her favorite rose bushes, my wife grew frustrated and took a trip to Home Depot. Soon she returned with a clever grin on her face and an innovative product in her hand called "Bag-A-Bug®."

It was pretty simple to set up. You just hang the bag—which includes a specially scented lure—in your yard and wait. Within minutes, these beetles, which were eating and mating with abandon, began to swarm to the bag. Once they got too close to the scented lure, it disoriented them and caused them to drop into the bag, trapped.

After a few days, the bag was so full that the metal stand began to bow due to the weight. It really was the strangest thing. Frankly, I know that bugs are a lower life form, but I expected that they would figure this thing out. Couldn't they see that the bugs just ahead of them quickly fell into the bag? Couldn't they hear the desperate buzzing of their fellow beetles in the bag and avoid the trap? But, alas for them, they did not, and soon there was not a single beetle left in our yard.

Well, it struck me that the Japanese beetles' behavior is an accurate metaphor for what happens to fathers who give into the enticement of pornography. Granted, from our perspective, the beetles were considered pests in the wrong place when they camped out on my wife's prized rose bushes. But these rose bushes were their home and where they were supposed to be. The bushes were a place for abundant sustenance and mating and were key to the beetles' survival. And yet they left it all for a temptation that trapped them and ultimately led to their death. Indeed, pornography is a kind of "Bag-A-Dad," and it can lead to a similar fate for any dad who gives in to its lure. At great cost, too many dads are failing to learn the lesson.

Pamela Paul, a *Times* magazine reporter and author of *Pornified*, documented:

> Today, the number of people looking at pornography is staggering. Americans rent upwards of 800 million pornographic videos and DVDs (about one in five of all rented movies is porn), and the 11,000 porn films shot each year far outpaces Hollywood's yearly slate of 400. Four billion dollars a year is spent on video pornography in the United States, more than on football, baseball, and basketball. One in four Internet users look at a pornography website in any given month. Men look at pornography online more than they look at any other subject. And 66 percent of 18–34-year-old men visit a pornographic site every month.[2]

In addition, a 2010 report, "The Social Costs of Pornography: A Statement of Findings and Recommendations," stated: "Unlike at any other time in history, pornography is now available and consumed widely in our society, due in large part to the Internet. No one remains untouched by it."[3]

Alas, despite the abundance of research about the perils of pornography, some fathers, even professing Christians, maintain the view that "a little porn on the side" never hurt anyone. But this is a very misguided and dangerous perspective. Pornography is a form of passive abuse that can irreparably damage a marriage and negatively impact one's ability to be a loving and engaged father. It can turn a father into a "Dr. Jekyll and Mr. Hyde" who can quickly lose control. You see, pornography creates a powerful "arousal addiction," which is very different than a drug addiction.[4] With a drug addiction, you want more of the same. However, with an arousal addiction, you want more of something different, and over time, this appetite and lust for variety will crowd out any desire for your wife and any connection to your children.

In the end, a father who consistently gives in to this temptation will find that he is no longer in control of his pornography addiction. His addiction will control him, leading him down a path of destruction, and eventually destroying him and all that he holds dear. Satan, the father of temptation, comes like a roaring lion to steal, kill, and destroy. Satan's goal is to blind a father to consequences of his behavior and to hinder him from being all that God intends for him to be. Pastor Bill Perkins, in his excellent book *When Good Men Are Tempted*, says, "A man controlled by his flesh (his sinful desires) is incapable of obeying God."[5] Indeed, a father must choose whom he will serve. He can choose to satisfy himself or to satisfy God by fulfilling the role that he was given.

Ironically, pornography, at its core, is not about providing satisfaction. It's about stoking *dissatisfaction*. Every picture and video is designed to make a man dissatisfied with the wife that God has given him and the responsibility for the children that God has entrusted to him. The more dissatisfied a father is, the better, because this means that he will consume more and more pornography. After all, for Hugh Hefner and his allies, it's just business.

LITTLE SHOP OF HORRORS

A popular musical called *Little Shop of Horrors* presents an entertaining and accurate allegory of how temptations like pornography work. The main character in the musical is Seymour Krelborn, a hapless and obscure fellow, who works at a skid row flower shop. He is frustrated with his lot in life, and the only bright spot is a pretty blonde woman named Audrey, who works at the shop as well. Seymour is in love with Audrey, but although she is nice to him, to his great disappointment, she shows no romantic interest in him.

Well, Seymour is walking along one day, and he comes across a small mysterious plant that looks like a Venus flytrap. He decides to keep the plant, and due to his love for Audrey, he decides to name the plant "Audrey II." He takes the plant to the flower shop. Despite giving it plenty of sunlight and water, it fails to thrive, but one day he accidentally pricks his finger on one of the plant's thorns, and the pod opens and starts making a sucking motion, much like a baby when it wants to nurse. Seymour quickly realizes what the plant wants and gives it a few drops of his blood. The tiny plant perks up immediately and sucks vigorously on Seymour's finger and starts to grow. So Seymour nurses the plant to vigor and health on a daily diet of his own blood.

As the plant grows, because of its unique appearance, people come from far and wide to see it. With the increased traffic and notoriety, the flower shop's business begins to pick up rapidly. Being Audrey II's owner, Seymour quickly becomes a celebrity as well, even attracting notice from Audrey, the desire of his heart. Seymour is hooked. He is addicted to the attention.

But soon a predictable problem arises. As Audrey II grows, the plant needs ever-increasing quantities of Seymour's blood. In fact,

Seymour now spends most of his waking hours feeding the plant. He is being sucked dry and his health is failing. So, reluctantly, he decides to stop feeding the plant.

However, when he cuts the plant off, Audrey II, to Seymour's astonishment, begins to speak. In an angry and booming voice, it demands to be fed. Failing at that, it seductively entices Seymour and tells him that it will help Seymour win Audrey's heart. Nevertheless, Seymour refuses to keep helping the plant.

Ultimately, he changes his mind when he witnesses Audrey's boyfriend abuse her. The plant cleverly uses Seymour's love for Audrey to its advantage, convincing Seymour that Audrey's abusive boyfriend would make good plant food. So Seymour sets out to kill the boyfriend. As fate would have it, the boyfriend accidentally kills himself, although Seymour could have intervened to prevent his death. In any case, Seymour feeds the boyfriend to the delighted plant.

As the musical progresses, the plant continues to make increasingly aggressive demands on Seymour, declaring, "Feed me!" In time, Seymour kills the shop owner and feeds him to the plant. Eventually the plant even kills Audrey and eats her too. Seymour does finally wise up and see the plant for the evil that it is, trying to kill the plant by shooting, cutting, and poisoning it. But, alas, it has grown too powerful. In the last scene, Seymour meets his sad and tragic fate. In an effort to finally free himself from this plant he once controlled, but that now controls him, he runs into its open jaws with a machete, hoping to kill the plant from inside. But this final attempt fails, and the plant eats him too.

There is an old saying about the difference between a habit and an addiction. A habit is something that you have. An addiction is something that has you. As Seymour learned, big addictions always start as small habits. But they can lead to one's destruction and death.

First Corinthians 10:13 tells us that no temptation has overtaken us that is not common to man. In short, temptation is common, presenting itself in predictable ways that a wise and disciplined father can avoid by pitching his family's tent far from it. However, too often, fathers fail, like Seymour, to heed the clear warning signs. The results can be disastrous, as we learn by examining the problems faced by Lot.

PITCHING A TENT NEAR TEMPTATION

Lot's story starts in earnest in Genesis 13. Lot and his uncle, Abraham, had been traveling together for some time, and each had developed very large herds of livestock. Consequently, a dispute arose between their herdsmen because there was limited grazing land. So Abraham said to Lot, "Let's not have any quarreling between you and me, or between your herders and mine, for we are close relatives" (Gen. 13:8). Telling Lot that they should split up, he allowed Lot to pick the direction that he would like to go, and Abraham would go in the opposite direction. Now Abraham's offer was a very generous one and reflected tremendous humility. As the eldest, he had the right to choose first, and Lot would have no choice but to take what Abraham didn't want.

Lot could have showed humility and, taking a cue from his name, offered to cast lots, but he didn't. He jumped at the chance to get the best for himself. He let the lust of his eyes be his guide, and he headed east. But there was a problem. Genesis 13:12 says that "Lot lived among the cities of the plain and pitched his tents near Sodom," a place where the men were wicked and great sinners against the Lord. Lot had pitched his family's tent near temptation.

Once Lot was gone, the Lord came to Abraham and again confirmed that he would bless him. God told Abraham, "All the land that you see I will give to you and your offspring forever" (Gen. 13:15). It's worth noting that Abraham headed *away* from Sodom, the land of temptation, and the first thing he did when he was settled was build an altar to the Lord.

The Bible doesn't say how long Lot lived near Sodom before he ran into problems. But when the problems started, they were major. You see, the king of Sodom and several other allied kings decided to rebel against a group of kings that had been ruling over them. The rebellious kings were quickly defeated, and the victorious kings took all of the losing kings' possessions. Unfortunately for Lot, he was in the wrong place at the wrong time, and he, his family, and his possessions were part of the booty. Lot had been overtaken due to his proximity to temptation and was suffering the painful consequences.

However, 1 Corinthians 10:13 reminds us that when temptation overtakes us, God is faithful, and he will also provide the way of escape. God did just that for Lot. When Abraham found out that Lot had been taken, he and a band of his trained men chased the kings that had taken Lot for about 150 miles. Abraham defeated the kings and brought back Lot, with his possessions and all of his people. Interestingly, Abraham met the king of Sodom and the king wanted to reward him. But Abraham refused to take anything from this king (Gen. 14).

Now, given Lot's miraculous rescue — his family and his possessions were returned to him — one would think that he would move as far as possible from Sodom. However, Lot did not. In a sense, Lot was "addicted" to Sodom. In fact, the next time that we read about Lot, he is sitting in the gateway of Sodom when two angels of the Lord come on their mission to destroy the city because of its wickedness (Gen. 19). And the conversation that Lot has with the angels provides an insight into the fact that Lot, despite God's earlier deliverance, has compromised to accommodate the temptations that surround him.

For example, when the angels said that they would spend the night in the town square, Lot insisted that they stay with him. Why? He was well aware of the wickedness of his surroundings and knew that the men of the city posed a danger to his guests. Also, he told the angels that they could rise up early to go on their way. But shouldn't he have wanted the angels of God to deal with the wickedness of the city? If not destroy it, at least Lot should have wanted them to redeem it. Furthermore, not only had he offered his daughters to be raped by the men of the city who had come to abuse his guests, but he had also allowed them to be engaged to marry men from Sodom. These men were so much a part of the wicked culture of the city that they laughed at Lot and refused to leave when he warned them of its impending destruction. And, finally, Lot lingered so much when it was time to leave that the angels had to seize him by the hand and lead him away to save his life.

However, one of the most disturbing results of Lot's decision to pitch his family's tent near temptation was what happened to his wife and daughters. Every child learns in Sunday school that Lot's wife turned to a pillar of salt because she failed to heed the angels' command not to look back at the burning Sodom and Gomorrah. But some of the blame for her sin must be laid at Lot's feet. First, the Bible says that Lot's wife was behind him. In my view, Lot should have been protecting his wife and she should have been in front of him. If she had been, when Lot saw her starting to look back, he could have warned her. Also, I suspect that she was afraid and felt vulnerable. If she had been in front of him, he would have been better positioned to encourage her and help her keep moving forward by reminding her that God would take care of them.

Second, as the head of his home, Lot chose to bring his wife to Sodom ... twice. He put her in the position to sin. A husband must not lead his wife into temptation. That's why when a husband gives in to the temptation of pornography, it is so damaging for his wife. It can leave her feeling unworthy, unloved, and longing for the intimacy and affection that her husband used to provide. It is a form of passive abuse that can lead his wife into temptation. It can make her vulnerable for an emotional and/or physical affair. Alas, she can end up "looking back" to past relationships and doubt whether her marriage to her husband is truly God's best for her. It's no wonder that there has been an increase in Facebook-initiated affairs as wives reconnect with old high school and college boyfriends.

When you consider what happened with Lot's daughters, there was a similar troubling dynamic. Faced with the prospect of the city's men wanting to have sex with the angels, Lot offered them his virgin daughters. How humiliating that must have been for his daughters, especially since they were engaged to be married. Assuredly, no man would want them after they had been violated in this way. Living in Sodom he had compromised their safety, and his own principles.

Again, as a result of Lot's choice to live in Sodom, he had to escape quickly, leaving all his possessions behind. Subsequently, he and his daughters ended up living in a cave. Separated from all society, his daughters became so afraid that they would never find husbands and have children that they got their father drunk and had sex with him. These choices also reflected the faulty morals they had developed while living in Sodom. The resulting two sons conceived by this incestuous union became the fathers of the Ammonites and the Moabites, peoples who would become perpetual enemies of the Israelites, the descendants of Abraham — the man who saved Lot's life.

So there is much that fathers can learn from Lot's story. He was a father who had been rescued, redeemed, and restored after succumbing to temptation, only to return to it again. In the end, his inability to resist temptation cost him his family, his wealth, and a godly legacy. That was a very high price to pay.

REFLECTION: THINK ON THESE THINGS

In this chapter, we focused on temptation in the area of pornography, a very serious issue that is destroying marriages and families. I urge fathers to address any challenges that they may have in this area aggressively and quickly. Please take a few moments to read and meditate on James 1:14 – 15: "But each person is tempted when they are dragged away by their own evil desire and enticed. Then, after desire has conceived, it gives birth to sin; and sin, when it is full-grown, gives birth to death." How does this passage apply to you?

CORRECTION: CHANGE THESE THINGS

When we succumb to temptation, God is faithful and, as in Lot's case, he can rescue, redeem, and restore us. However, to make sure that we don't return, it is important to understand the process that leads us to temptation in the first place.

In his book *When Good Men Are Tempted*, Pastor Bill Perkins uses the passage from James to outline four distinct steps that are part of an addictive cycle: Enticement (Preoccupation), Conception (Ritualization), Birth (Acting Out), and Death (Shame).

Pastor Perkins astutely offers that the key to freedom from an addictive cycle is to cut off temptation at the enticement stage. He says, "Nothing is more important for a man wanting to find freedom from sexual lust than identifying the rituals that precede an episode of acting out."[6]

Therefore, if you have an issue with a destructive habit, I would like you to take a moment and list your rituals — all of them. (Examples could be driving by a strip club, reading personal ads, visiting a specific Internet site.) Once you have done this, list specifically what you will do to avoid these rituals in the future.

Resisting pornography and sexual temptation is one of the most difficult challenges that many fathers face, especially if they don't get help. The good news is that there is a lot of help available. For example, I highly recommend Pastor Perkins's book and the *Every Man's Battle* series on sexual integrity. Also, there are a number of fantastic Internet filters to help you avoid pornography via the web. However, I believe that the most important thing that any father can do in this area is to become accountable to other fathers. James 5:16 says that we should confess our sins to one another and pray for one another, that we may be healed. Satan likes nothing more than a father who is isolated and struggling alone. That said, a great way to start on the road to accountability would be to share your list of rituals with a father or group of fathers that you trust. Ask them to hold you accountable to make sure that you don't return to past behavior. Remember, it's been said that discipline, not just desire, determines a man's destiny.

Finally, if you are married, I believe that it's very important to discuss this issue with your wife. After all, God has given her to you as a helpmate. Granted, the conversation may be difficult because she may view your struggles in this area as a reflection on her and/or a rejection of her. Accordingly, it's critical that you help her understand that you want her involvement because you love her so much. In fact, you may want her to read this chapter before you have the discussion.

CONNECTION: DO THIS THING

Now that you have reflected upon what God needs you to do to make sure that you don't pitch your family's tent near temptation, it's time for you to make the Good Dad Promise. You need to make this promise to God, to yourself, and to your wife (or the mother of your children), and to your children.

GOOD DAD

PROMISE #8

I will not pitch my family's tent near temptation.

CHAPTER TEN

6 THINGS A DAD MUST DO TO BE A GOOD FATHER

You call out to God for help and he helps—he's a good Father that way. But don't forget, he's also a responsible Father, and won't let you get by with sloppy living.

1 Peter 1:17 (MSG)

WHILE I WAS WRITING THIS BOOK, I experienced a personal tragedy. Jay Young, one of my best friends for over thirty years, died unexpectedly. It was a tough loss. We had been friends since our freshman year in college. In the days since Jay's death, I have thought quite a bit about what connected us because we had a lot in common. For example, we were both African American boys who grew up in midsize Midwestern towns. We both were avid football fans who played the game from our youth into our college years, and we both loved the Pittsburgh Steelers. Additionally, we both grew up with single mothers, and the absence of our fathers had much to do with the men that we later became: committed, married fathers with sons.

When someone close to you dies, it's not uncommon to have regrets and long to have just one more opportunity to spend time with them. Jay and I were both busy guys with busy lives, and I certainly have some of these feelings. But, interestingly, since his passing, most of my thoughts about Jay have been related to the conversations that we had about fatherhood. This was a defining aspect of our relationship. We both wanted the "secret sauce" formula to be good fathers. This spilled over into my commitment to helping other men grow as fathers.

Not surprisingly, when I was president of National Fatherhood Initiative, one of the most frequent questions that I got from fathers was, "What do I need to do to make sure that I am a good dad?" Great question. Well, for starters, a father needs to avoid the eight "bad dad" mistakes that were discussed earlier in this book. However, being a good father is not just about what you *don't* do. It's also about what you *do*. So to help you on your journey to be the good dad God desires you to be, I have outlined six things that every good father must do.

1. GOOD FATHERS AFFIRM THEIR CHILDREN

Several years ago, I was preparing to speak about fatherhood at a men's prayer breakfast and I wasn't quite sure what to say. I needed a fresh word from God. So I started thumbing through my Bible and came across Matthew 3:13–4:1.

Then Jesus came from Galilee to the Jordan to be baptized by John. But John tried to deter him, saying, "I need to be baptized by you, and do you come to me?"

Jesus replied, "Let it be so now; it is proper for us to do this to fulfill all righteousness." Then John consented.

As soon as Jesus was baptized, he went up out of the water. At that moment heaven was opened, and he saw the Spirit of God descending like a dove and alighting on him. And a voice from heaven said, "This is my Son, whom I love; with him I am well pleased."

Then Jesus was led by the Spirit into the wilderness to be tempted by the devil.

Having been a Christian for a long time, I had read this passage many times, but now it struck me anew. As I considered what was happening here, God gave me this notion of "affirmation before temptation." You see, here was Jesus — fully God and fully man — but God the Father knew that in Jesus' humanity, it was important that he received his Father's affirmation.

The timing of this affirmation was significant. First, Jesus was about to set out into the world on the mission for which he came to earth. The words of the affirmation confirmed Jesus' identity, purpose, and destiny. Second, Jesus was about to enter a time of tremendous temptation. Matthew 4:1 – 11 tells the story of how Satan tried to tempt Jesus in three ways: "lust of the flesh" or the desire to enjoy, "lust of the eye" or the desire to obtain, "the pride of life" or the desire to accomplish. And, as we know, Jesus faced all of these temptations and did not sin.[1]

Note this: everything that Satan tried to use as temptations were imitations of the real thing and were things that Jesus already possessed under his dominion. He had true "enjoyment" through his relationship with God the Father. He had "obtained" all that

167

there was through his relationship with God the Father. He was sure to "accomplish" the most important task of all creation when he died on the cross and took the sins of all humanity onto his shoulders. You see, Jesus had a divine clarity when he faced Satan's temptation. The Father had affirmed him, so he knew *who* he was and *whose* he was. Once you know the real thing, no imitation will do.

So, in this passage about the baptism and temptation of Jesus, God the Father has modeled one of the key actions that every earthly father should emulate. That is, a father must affirm his children. Why? Because one thing that we know for sure is the tempter will come — in one form or another. You may recall that I believe a child has a "hole in his soul" in the shape of his dad. Well, this is the exact place where a father's affirmation is supposed to go. If a father is unable or unwilling to affirm his child and fill this void, Satan is sure to try and fill it with imitations of God's goodness, just like he tried to do with Jesus.

Now, consider for a moment how a father's failure to affirm his children manifests itself in our world. Our news headlines are filled with stories about adults and children who have caused tremendous harm to themselves and others because they never heard their fathers say, "This is my son (or this is my daughter), whom I love; I am well pleased." No doubt, every pimp, drug dealer, gang leader, and those who would encourage our kids to sell their bodies and forfeit their souls knows how to tap into the void left by absent fathers. Remember, DC sniper Lee Malvo's words, "He [Muhammad] knew exactly what motivated me, what I longed for, what was lacking ... I couldn't say 'no.'"[2] But when our kids are affirmed, they know *who* they are and *whose* they are. Then, like Jesus, they won't settle for anything less than the real thing, and, like Jesus, they will be able to say "no" to the temptations of the Evil One and "yes" to the will of God.

A few weeks after Jay's funeral, I called his son to see how he was doing. We talked for a long time about his father. This young man clearly missed his dad a great deal. As I listened to him share his heart, I could not help but wonder about what lies ahead for him. He is about to enter the tumultuous teen years, a time when the guiding hand of a good father is especially needed. Although I can never replace his dad, I am committed to do what I can to help this young man navigate successfully through this important time. I must admit that I was initially a bit worried. However, as we were ending the conversation, he said something that gave me a confidence that everything was going to be just fine. He said, "My father was a hero to me. The look of approval on his face was better than any trophy that I could ever receive."

You see, in the years before his death, Jay had invested mightily in his young son's life to make sure his son knew *who* he was and *whose* he was. That's the power of affirmation before temptation. That's the power and influence of a good dad.

2. GOOD FATHERS ARE PHYSICALLY PRESENT

Most fathers that I speak with understand that they need to financially provide for their children. Providing is such a well-understood aspect of fathering that often a dad is just referred to as "the provider." In fact, I often tell people that this is the only way that the government tends to think about dads. Alas, while there are a plethora of programs for women focused on maternal health and child well-being, for years, there have been just two for fathers: the tax code for married fathers and child support enforcement for unmarried fathers. Basically, from the government's perspective, if a father is paying for his children, then he is a good father. Interestingly, this viewpoint has spread throughout our culture, with some unfortunate and unexpected consequences, especially for low-income, unemployed, and under-employed fathers. Some of these dads actually believe that they can't be good fathers and really have nothing to offer to their children if they don't have a paycheck of a certain size.

Prior to working for National Fatherhood Initiative, I spent nearly twenty years in corporate America, and I saw dads who viewed their fathering solely through the "provider" lens. They would spend countless hours at work — missing key milestones in their children's lives — laboring under the misguided notion that the more money they made, the better fathers they were. Ironically, their lack of work and family balance was an obstacle rather than a facilitator to their efforts to be good dads. In fact, National Fatherhood Initiative's research shows that fathers cite work responsibilities as the number one obstacle that prevents them from being the dads that they desire to be.[3]

But good fathering is less about the "presents" that money can buy than your "presence," which no amount of money can replace. Kids spell love T-I-M-E, and they come out of the womb with an instinctive understanding that time is your most valuable asset. Let's face it. Whether you are Donald Trump or Donald Dump, you only get twenty-four hours in a day and 365 days in a year. You can't barter for or buy one second more.

When I first became a dad, I had an epiphany about how important it is for fathers to consider time from a child's perspective. My oldest son Jamin was just about a year old and I was a new marketing representative in training at IBM. As part of the training process, several times during my first year, I had to spend about three to four weeks away from home taking sales and marketing classes.

After one of these trips, I was pretty amazed at how much my young son had changed in just a few weeks. Then it hit me. Kid time and adult time are very different in a relative sense. For example, if a baby is just two days old and you miss one day, you have missed 50 percent of his or her life. For you, one day is just a tiny fraction of your life. The bottom line is, in a relative sense, when you miss time in your child's life, it means a lot more to them than it may to you. But the flip side is also true. When you give them your time, it means more to them than you may realize.

Given the above, why do so many dads who want to be good fathers embrace such a narrow view of what it means to provide? Well, I believe that it may be due to a limited perspective of Matthew 7:9, which I discussed in the introduction. In this verse, Jesus asked a group of fathers an interesting rhetorical question. He said, "Which of you, if your son asked for bread, will give him a stone?" He goes on to say these fathers know how to give their kids good things.

Over the years, I have used this verse often to encourage fathers to be good dads — those who give their children bread — rather than "bad dads" — those who give their children stones. It's clear this verse illustrates this important principle. However, in Matthew 4:4, in the midst of his temptation, Jesus says, "Man shall not live on bread alone, but on every word that comes from the mouth of God." In other words, providing a material good is necessary, but it's not sufficient. Good dads, like our good heavenly Father, do more because they know kids need more. They need dads who don't just give *of* themselves. They need dads who give *themselves* as well.

171

3. GOOD FATHERS ARE EMOTIONALLY AVAILABLE

Be honest, when you think of the word *nurture* in the context of parenting, who comes to mind? If you are like most dads, the answer is "mom." That's understandable, because the origin of the word *nurture* is "to feed or provide nourishment," which, of course, brings to mind the image of a mother breastfeeding her newborn. Also, most of the time when people talk about nurturing, it's in the context of mothering. Moreover, parenting is often framed in a "good cop/bad cop" paradigm where mothers nurture and fathers discipline. However, nurturing is not just "women's work." Nurturing entails more aspects than you think, and I want to challenge you to think about what it means to nurture in broader terms.

So what is nurturing? It means supporting and being involved in *every* aspect of your child's growth and development. In addition, it means that you are in tune with the emotional well-being of your child. You don't "outsource" this to mom. Yes, I know that the emotional world of children, especially as they move into the teen years, can be imprecise, complicated, and messy, but you have to "go there" if you want to be a good dad. Remember, there is no intimacy without vulnerability. And a father is never more vulnerable than when he is nurturing his child. After all, Malachi 4:6 makes it clear that God's desire is for the hearts of fathers to be connected to the hearts of their children. This can only happen if fathers are nurturers.

The good news is that in the Bible there are countless Scriptures where God, as a loving Father, promises to nurture us and meet us at our point of need. For example, Psalm 55:22 says, "Cast your cares on the LORD and he will sustain you; he will never let the righteous be shaken." What an excellent example for fathers! When you are vested in the emotional well-being of your children, you sustain them during the very challenging times in their lives.

And there is more good news. You see, we can glean some very practical instances of ways we can nurture our children by examining how God the Father nurtured his Son, Jesus. Below are some good examples:

He listened to Jesus. In Matthew 6:9–13, Jesus teaches his disciples how to pray by giving them the "Lord's Prayer." Prior to giving them the prayer, he tells them, "But when you pray, go into your room, close the door and pray to your Father, who is unseen. Then your Father, who sees what is done in secret, will reward you" (Matt. 6:6). Indeed, prayer is a special time when God is listening to us. Based on Jesus' comments, we have blessed assurance that when we pray, he's "all ears."

He protected Jesus. In his humanity, Jesus was in his most vulnerable state when he was an infant. You may recall that Herod sought to kill Jesus, but he could not because an angel of the Lord told Joseph in a dream to take Mary and the baby Jesus to Egypt (Matt. 2). Good fathers always protect their children from physical, emotional, and spiritual harm.

He comforted Jesus. When Jesus was under great distress because he knew that he would have to die a painful death on the cross, he went to the garden of Gethsemane to pray. Why? Because he found comfort in the presence of God the Father. Indeed, good fathers are comforters for their children.

He met Jesus at his point of need. Matthew 4:1–11 chronicles the temptation of Jesus. He had just completed fasting for forty days and nights, and he was clearly at his weakest physically. After he resisted all of Satan's temptations, the Bible says that "angels came and attended him" (v. 11). Attending is all about addressing a person's needs, and good fathers always look for opportunities to do this for their children.

Modeling your behavior as a nurturing father after the simple and doable actions above is sure to yield a wonderful return in your relationship with your children. No doubt, because you are more emotionally available, you and your kids will be connected heart to heart.

Likewise, the reverse is also true. Unpleasant consequences are almost certain to result when a father places a low priority on nurturing. I used to work in finance. Over the years, I have been amazed at how similar some financial concepts are to fatherhood principles. One concept that I have found particularly useful is the notion that dads need to make regular "deposits" into their children's "emotional bank accounts," a concept that the late Dr. Stephen R. Covey discusses in his fantastic book, *The 8th Habit: From Effectiveness to Greatness*.[4] After all, chances are one day — like when your daughter wants to date the "wrong" guy or your son wants to tattoo his latest girlfriend's name across his forehead — you may need to make a huge "withdrawal." So I thought it appropriate to end this section with an imaginary conversation involving a father who failed to "invest" in nurturing his teenage daughter.

(*Scene* — Dad rushes into the lobby of the First National Bank of his fifteen-year-old daughter's heart and quickly approaches her window.)

> *Daughter:* Good afternoon. How may I help you?
> *Dad:* Hi. I need to make a big withdrawal fast!
> *Daughter:* Okay, sir. No problem. Could you please let me see some ID?

Dad: Sure. (Dad hands her a copy of her birth certificate where he is listed as "Father.")

Daughter: Everything looks in order, Dad. Please wait just a minute while I check your account. (She turns away from him and checks her computer, but then she gets a rather concerned look on her face.)

Dad: Is there a problem?

Daughter: Yes, sort of. I clearly see you opened an account here a long time ago, but it doesn't appear to have a sufficient balance for you to make a big withdrawal. When was the last time that you made a deposit?

Dad: Well, I don't remember. I guess it's been a while. You know, I have been very busy working and stuff like that. But my wife has been making lots of deposits. Seems like every time I turn around she is heading here. Frankly, it's like a daily thing for her. Since we are married, can't I just make a withdrawal from her account?

Daughter: No, you can't, because we don't offer joint accounts here.

Dad: Oh yeah ... That's right ... I remember hearing that. What about a loan? Can I get one of those?

Daughter: I'm sorry ... We don't offer loans either. You can only withdraw what you have deposited.

Dad (starting to get a bit upset): Well, that just doesn't seem fair! I clearly have an account ... And, well, I need to make a withdrawal ... Can't you make an exception? After all, I am DAD.

Daughter: Dad, I am sorry ... I just can't help you....

Dad (becoming more upset, raising his voice): Well, doggone it, I am not going to take no for an answer.

(The daughter gets a very frustrated and stern look on her face, and she starts to reach under the counter to push the button for security.)

> *Daughter:* As I said, I can't help you. You knew the rules when you opened the account. How can you expect to withdraw funds that you didn't deposit? That's just not the way it works here ... All you had to do was make consistent deposits ... Even small ones would have been fine because interest—your interest in my life—would have compounded these deposits substantially over time. Taking deposits that don't belong to you is ... well, robbery. So I need to ask you to leave now. Or do I need to call security?[5]

4. GOOD FATHERS ARE SPIRITUALLY INVOLVED

In the first chapter of this book, I wrote quite a bit about why fathers must be spiritually involved in their children's lives, and how their lack of involvement can be a key barrier to their children coming to faith in Jesus Christ. Now I want to give you a model for how fathers should be spiritually involved in their children's lives.

Recently, I was reading about the increase in the number of people who want to climb Mount Everest. Apparently, this has become a very big business as thrill seekers, young and old, experienced and novice, covet the opportunity to put their bodies and minds to the ultimate test. After all, Mount Everest, which is located in the Himalayas on the border between China and Nepal, is the earth's highest mountain with its peak at an amazing 29,029 feet above sea level.

Two standard routes are used by most climbers, and neither poses a significant technical challenge. Nonetheless, Mount Everest presents a number of dangers, including temperatures that are frigid enough to cause frostbite and monsoon-category high winds. In addition, climbers have a limited number of months in the year to make their attempt, along with very tight time periods during the day to safely ascend and descend the mountain. But the most dangerous obstacle, and the one that has caused most of the climber deaths, is altitude sickness. This condition, which is caused by the low availability of oxygen, can start at just eight thousand feet above sea level. In its most severe case, it causes fluid on the lungs and swelling on the brain that will leave a person so disoriented that they can't think clearly. If this happens to you while on Mount Everest, it means almost certain death.

You see, the other climbers, who tend to be focused on reaching the summit and their own survival, have limited oxygen to spare and not much time to help you. Moreover, especially if you have a problem on the descent, they won't have the strength to bring you down the mountain without putting their own lives at risk. In fact, what happened to climber David Sharp illustrates this point well. In 2006, on Sharp's third attempt, he is believed to have finally reached Mount Everest's summit, but on the way down, became exhausted and ran out of oxygen. At least forty climbers passed him, but no one made an attempt to rescue him. Alone, out of oxygen, and severely frostbitten, he died in a cave next to the corpse known as "Green Boots," twenty-eight-year-old Indian climber Tsewang Paljorto, whose frozen, undisturbed body had served ten years as both a marker and a warning of what could await ill-prepared climbers.[6]

Therefore, it's not surprising that even the most experienced climbers don't venture to tackle Mount Everest alone. In fact, they hire special guides called "Sherpas." The Sherpas are a unique people who, for generations, have inhabited the Khumbu Valley, the national park surrounding Everest. Because they have been living in the area for so long, they have developed a genetic ability to function at very high altitudes. Whereas most people start to have oxygen problems above eight thousand feet, they have an amazing endurance up to about twenty-three thousand feet. Since the Sherpa guides have trekked Everest many times, they are experts when it comes to knowing the weather patterns and the best time to climb. Moreover, the Sherpas are adept at pointing out the Green Boots and perils because they are well aware of the consequences that await those who fail to heed their warning. (Of note, David Sharp did not hire a Sherpa. He chose to climb alone.[7])

But these gifted Sherpa guides can do something else that is wondrously important. With their uniquely trained and experienced eyes, they can help those in their care pause and take in the beauty of Mount Everest. You see, this mountain is not all danger. It's a delight as well, with many breathtaking peaks, vistas, and valleys that one can only see from its heights. That's why so many are drawn to it and would risk life and limb to plant their personal flag on its summit. And it's not surprising that the official Tibetan name for Mount Everest is Chomolungma, which means "Holy Mother."

As I reflect upon what I had learned about Mount Everest and the Sherpa guides, it struck me that this was a fantastic metaphor for good fathers who seek to be spiritually involved in their children's lives. Parenting has much in common with climbing Mount Everest; children need their fathers, like inexperienced climbers need the Sherpas, to guide them and to help them avoid the perils and unwise decisions of life. But they also need their fathers to help them appreciate the wonders that await them on the upward journey to fulfill God's purpose for their lives. You see, good dads are "guide dads."

But there is a problem.

Although Sherpas are born at a high altitude, which uniquely prepares them to be effective guides, fathers are not born "acclimated" to be spiritual guides for their children. They can only reach the spiritual high altitudes of a close relationship with God through praying, fasting, and studying Scripture. Only then can a father truly get the wisdom and discernment necessary to guide his children properly. Without wisdom from God, a father will be an ill-equipped and unprepared blind guide who won't be able to see spiritual dangers that his children must avoid. He also will not be able to help his children see God's blessings in the peaks and valleys of life.

So if a father truly wants to be spiritually involved and guide his children, here are four key things that he must do:

Develop a strong relationship with God. A father must "practice what he preaches" and be disciplined in spending daily time with God in prayer and reading the Bible. As Paul exhorted Timothy, "All Scripture is God-breathed and is useful for teaching, rebuking, correcting and training in righteousness, so that the servant of God may be thoroughly equipped for every good work" (2 Tim. 3:16–17). Given the distractions of life, I know that daily prayer and Bible reading can be a challenge. But you can't give what you don't have, and you can't guide your children on a spiritual journey that you have never taken.

Pray daily for and with your children. Ephesians 6:12 says, "For

179

our struggle is not against flesh and blood, but against the rulers, against the authorities, against the powers of this dark world and against the spiritual forces of evil in the heavenly realms." A father must never forget that there is a war going on, and prayer is the most important weapon in his arsenal. Remember, there is an Evil One and a culture that would like nothing more than to lead your children off a cliff.

Model the spiritual behavior that you want to see. The notion of "do as I say but not as I do" has never worked. It's the essence of hypocrisy, and children detect this right away. Remember that your children are more likely to "be what they see." That said, the most important behavior that you must model is love, not just toward your children and family, but also toward people that you may not like. Note what 1 Corinthians 13:3–8 says about love:

> If I give all I possess to the poor and give over my body to hardship that I may boast, but do not have love, I gain nothing.
>
> Love is patient, love is kind. It does not envy, it does not boast, it is not proud. It does not dishonor others, it is not self-seeking, it is not easily angered, it keeps no record of wrongs. Love does not delight in evil but rejoices with the truth. It always protects, always trusts, always hopes, always perseveres.
>
> Love never fails.

Set spiritual "markers" to help your children stay on the path. When climbers make the trek up Everest, there are many markers and landmarks that they use to help them stay on the right path while heading to the summit. Some markers, like Green Boots, are quite poignant, but others, like planted flags, are signs of hope and are a tremendous source of encouragement, especially when the climbers are weary. First Samuel 7:1–13 chronicles the story of how the Israelites were afraid of an approaching Philistine army. All seemed lost, but God delivered them. To mark this deliverance, Samuel set a special stone called an "Ebenezer." He wanted the Israelites to never forget "thus far the LORD has helped us" (v. 12). I believe that Samuel's action serves as a great example for fathers. In fact, I know a dad who actually buys stones and engraves them with important dates and occasions when God has met his family's needs. He told me that he wants visual reminders for his children so that they will know that there is a God who will always help them.

5. GOOD FATHERS LOVE AND PURSUE THE PRODIGAL CHILD

Recently I read a *Christianity Today* article that featured an interview with pastor and author John Piper, giving his thoughts about the importance of reconciliation. At the end of the interview, he talked about how his son walked away from the Christian faith at age nineteen. He said: "I was pursuing him constantly ... emailing every day almost, taking him to lunch every time he came back to town, trying not to preach at him. Everything in me wanted this kid back."[8]

As I read John Piper's words, I was reminded of the story of the prodigal son in Luke 15:11 – 32. Here was a father who had two sons, and one day the younger son came to his father and asked for his inheritance. The father complied, and to the father's regret, this younger son left home. And, like Piper, everything in this father wanted his son back.

Over the years, I have heard many sermons on this parable, and all of them have used it to illustrate how much our heavenly Father loves us and desires to restore us to himself, no matter what we have done. The Bible says that we all have sinned and fallen short of the glory of God (Rom. 3:23). Therefore, we are all prodigals. However, as a father, I could not help but think about how it must have felt to have a child that you love essentially reject you and all that you value. You see, the prodigal son valued what his father had, but he didn't value who his father was and what his father valued. Like John Piper's son, the prodigal son was an unbeliever.

Now, I raise this point because in the previous sections, I have written about what a good father does. As men, we like systems, equations, and formulas that can be solved to get the right answer and a certain fixed conclusion. Therefore, we can easily fall into the trap of believing that if we follow certain steps, our children are guaranteed to be what we want them to be. This is a logical conclusion. But, unfortunately, fathering—even the best— doesn't work this way. Think about it. The father in the story of the prodigal son represents God, the ultimate Good Father. Yet his son rejects him and goes his own way.

So, should fathers despair? Of course not. Years ago, a wise Christian told me something that I would never forget. He said, "You take care of the effort, and God will take care of the results." From a fatherhood perspective, this means that a dad just needs to make sure that he is faithfully doing his best to follow Proverbs 22:6, training up his children in the way they should go so that when they are old, they won't depart from it.

That said, I believe one of the reasons God made sure this story was in the Bible was to illustrate an important truth for fathers. Sometimes, despite a father's best efforts, a child may decide to go down an unwise path. When God created man and gave him free will, he knew that by giving man the ability to run *to* him, he was also giving man the ability to run *from* him. This is true also for every father who brings a child into the world. Remember, our heavenly Father wants us to love him. But one cannot truly love another unless one has the freedom to *not* love as well.

I believe God also placed this passage in the Bible as a model of two important principles that fathers must remember should they have a prodigal child. The first principle is that a father must demonstrate a steadfast love. No doubt, when a child has acted out badly, rejecting you and many of the values that you consider sacred, it can be very difficult to continue to demonstrate love. But, as 1 Corinthians 13:1 makes clear, without love the words that you speak to your prodigal child will sound to him or her like a "resounding gong or a clanging cymbal." You see, love bears all things, believes all things, hopes all things, and endures all things. A father, like the one in the prodigal son story, rises early in the morning—day after day—and looks to the horizon with an abiding hope that today might just be the day when my child will return. A father will only have the ability and discipline to do this if he has a steadfast love for his prodigal.

The second principle is the notion of helping your other children learn the right lessons from the behavior of the prodigal son. For example, if the prodigal son story was in today's setting, this son would post frequent updates on Facebook, YouTube, and Twitter with pictures and videos showing your other children just how much fun he was having. Assuredly, his behavior would do one of two things. It would either tempt your other children to follow in his footsteps, or it would create resentment and jealousy toward the prodigal child and fill your other children's hearts with a self-righteous pride. In fact, you may recall that the latter is exactly what happened to the older brother in the story of the prodigal son. When the loving father threw a party to celebrate the return of his younger son, the older brother became enraged with his father. The older brother must have felt like he was a real "sucker" for doing the right thing for all those years while his brother partied away. It would be easy for him to conclude he had labored in vain.

Therefore, how the father responded to the older brother would be extremely critical. It would be important that this father remember that our battle is not against flesh and blood. There is an Evil One who seeks to steal, kill, and destroy. He wants to steal your faith *and* your children from you, kill your relationship with them, and destroy the unity that exists between your children.

It's clear that the father in the prodigal son story was very aware of the family dynamics at play. He needed to respond to the older brother in a way that affirmed him and still demonstrated love for his wayward brother. Moreover, he could not leave the impression that there are no consequences for sin. Note what he says in Luke 15:31–32: "My son ... you are always with me, and everything I have is yours. But we had to celebrate and be glad, because this brother of yours was dead and is alive again; he was lost and is found."

His comments reflect the perfect balance between justice and mercy. You see, when he tells his son "everything I have is yours," he is reminding the older son that the younger son has lost his inheritance, so there is a just consequence for his behavior. He is reminding the older brother of the principle illustrated by Galatians 6:9, which says, "Let us not become weary in doing good, for at the proper time we will reap a harvest if we do not give up."

However, this father was also modeling for the older brother the importance of mercy, which he would not have been able to do if he did not truly have a steadfast love for the younger brother. (That's why maintaining one's love for the prodigal child is so critical!) Mercy is showing compassion and kindness toward an offender or another person in one's power. Given the family dynamics and what the younger son had done, the older brother would clearly be in control, and the father wanted to model how he was to treat his younger brother after the father was gone, much like Christ modeled for us how we were to treat each other after he was gone. You see, this wise and loving father wasn't just seeking to restore his younger son to himself; he was also seeking to restore the relationship between these two brothers, because that is what good fathers do. Love hopes all things.

Well, at this point, you are probably wondering what happened in the case of John Piper's son. Good news and glory to God, his prodigal son returned home as well. In the interview Piper said: "He came back to the Lord four years later and the church had a beautiful, beautiful restoration service. He wept his eyes out in front the church and was restored."[9]

Indeed, love hopes all things.

In fact, Piper's son wrote a wonderful article that you can find on Pastor Piper's Desiring God website, where he outlines ways to love your wayward child.[10] It will give you some excellent advice and practice steps to help you live out the principles that have been discussed in this section. Remember, love rejoices with the truth. And love never ends.

6. GOOD FATHERS REACH OUT TO THE FATHERLESS

God truly cares about the fatherless. Depending on which translation you read, the word *fatherless* is mentioned over forty times in the Bible. In fact, in Psalm 68:5, God is described as the "father to the fatherless." Moreover, Deuteronomy 10:18 says that God "defends the cause of the fatherless." Therefore, it certainly stands to reason that if God, the ultimate Good Father whom every dad should use as a model, cares so deeply about the fatherless, any father who wants to be a good one should as well. Accordingly, God has impressed upon my heart that a good father provides for, nurtures, and guides his own children, *and* he must proactively seek to be a role model and mentor for other children who lack a father's love and guidance.

There is a wonderful example of this principle in the life of David recounted in 2 Samuel 9. You may recall that David and Jonathan, King Saul's son, shared a special friendship. In fact, when Saul sought to unjustly kill David, Jonathan tried to protect David, even to the point of risking his own life. However, Jonathan was eventually killed in battle, leaving behind a son named Mephibosheth, who had been made a cripple when a nurse dropped him. When David became king, he found this young man and gave him all that had belonged to Saul. Moreover, he declared that Mephibosheth would forevermore eat at the king's table. Now, David certainly made a "bad dad" mistake in his dealings with his sons Amnon and Absalom, but in this case, David truly demonstrated that he was a man after God's heart by becoming a father to the fatherless Mephibosheth.

Several years ago, in my work with National Fatherhood Initiative, I coined a term that reflects the principle of what David did. I called it being a "Double-Duty Dad." In fact, we developed a program, which includes free downloadable resources, designed to help dads truly live out this important aspect of fathering.[11] Why? Because Double-Duty Dads are needed now more than ever. Tonight, twenty-five million kids — one out of three children—will go to bed in a home where their father does not reside. Moreover, according to the National Mentoring Partnership, nearly eighteen million kids want or need mentoring, yet only three million of these children are able to get mentors.[12] And the vast majority of the mentors are women.

You are probably saying about now, "I have my hands full with my own kids ... How could I possibly sign up to be a mentor to someone else's child?" Well, that's the beauty of the Double-Duty Dad concept. It doesn't require you to sign up for anything. You don't have to "look out" but rather "look down and around," like David did, to positively impact a child who is within your own "circle of influence." So the fatherless child that you reach out to could be a niece or nephew, your next-door neighbor's kids, someone from your church's youth group, or a kid on a youth sports team that you coach for your children. If they are nearby, you can easily and intentionally include this child into activities that you are already doing with your children. If they live far away, something as simple as a weekly call or periodic notes of encouragement would be easy for you to do, but they mean so much to a vulnerable child in need.

Again, remember how John Muhammad was able to get young Lee Malvo under his deadly sway. Kids who don't have Double-Duty Dads are easy prey for "double-dangerous dads." Accordingly, a small commitment on your part could change a child's life forever and save the lives of countless people that you will never know.

Early in this chapter I mentioned that my good friend Jay passed away suddenly and left behind a twelve-year-old son. I have committed to be a Double-Duty Dad for this young boy. Think about it. He is within my circle of influence, and I am uniquely positioned to speak into his life and help him on his important journey to manhood. Of course, I am not seeking to replace his father. No one can. But as a father, I can continue to show him what a father's love looks and feels like.

I have been a father for nearly three decades, and the skills that I have developed are transferable to this mentoring relationship. I have even learned from the mistakes that I have made, and he will benefit from these lessons. Moreover, the research suggests that for mentoring relationships to be effective, they must be maintained over a long period of time—at least a year—or it can actually be damaging for children.[13] This certainly won't be a problem with my mentoring relationship with Jay's son. Also, it's extremely helpful if the mentor has a good relationship with their mentee's primary caregiver, which is usually the child's mother. In this case, I have known Jay's widow for many years, and she is very supportive of my commitment to spend time with her son.

The bottom line is that being a Double-Duty Dad is something that every father can do, and I believe that mentoring the fatherless is something that God calls every father to do. There are sixty-five million fathers in America. Just imagine what would happen in our churches, schools, neighborhoods, and communities if an "army" of good fathers reached out to fatherless children in this way! After all, every good dad has something that every fatherless child desperately needs. They have a wellspring of experiences and knowledge that has been invaluable for their own children. Moreover, simply by being intentional and including a fatherless child in some of the activities that they do with their children, they can help break the long-term cycle of father absence and the negative outcomes that fatherless children disproportionately face. A Double-Duty Dad does the sacred and God-honoring work of modeling what it means to be an involved, responsible, and committed godly father—someone that a boy can be inspired to be and that a girl can be inspired to look for in a husband and her children's father.

REFLECTION: THINK ON THESE THINGS

You probably noticed that this chapter on how to be a good father is the longest one in the book. That's not by accident. I wanted to make sure that you understand that "bad dad" mistakes don't have to define you as a father. Every dad makes mistakes. They are not who you are. They are what you did. So, if you have made some of these mistakes, you should not lose heart. You should learn from your mistakes and commit to keep your "good dad" promise going forward. As many of the fathers featured in the book knew well, we serve a God of second chances who stands by to help us be the fathers that we long to be. You must always remember that your fathering can be transformed by the renewing of your mind and a renewed commitment to follow God's principles.

That said, I would like you to take a few moments and review the list below of six things that good fathers do. Which of these things have you been doing well? Which have been the most challenging for you?

1. Good Fathers Affirm Their Children
2. Good Fathers Are Physically Present
3. Good Fathers Are Emotionally Available
4. Good Fathers Are Spiritually Involved
5. Good Fathers Love and Pursue the Prodigal Child
6. Good Fathers Reach Out to the Fatherless

CORRECTION: CHANGE THESE THINGS

Now that you have reflected on the list above, I would like you to start by picking the area that has been the most challenging for you. Then I would like you to list three specific actions that you will take this week to address this issue. Then I would like you to do the same thing for each of the areas that you have listed as a challenge. So, if you have been "outsourcing" the spiritual development of your children to their mother, make a change now. If you have a prodigal child that you have not been pursuing, make the change now. If you have not reached out to a fatherless child in your circle of influence, make the change now. You can start by visiting www.fatherhood.org/doubledutydad to learn more about how easy it is to be a Double-Duty Dad and to download a free resource to help you get started. You should also encourage other good fathers that you know to become Double-Duty Dads as well. You could even start a Double-Duty Dad group so that you and the other dads can have a specific place to support each other and those you mentor.

CONNECTION: DO THIS THING

Now that you have reflected upon what God needs you to do, and made a plan to correct any "bad dad" mistakes, and committed to live out the six things that good fathers do, you need to make one final promise to God, to yourself, to your wife (or the mother of your children), and to your children.

GOOD
DAD

PROMISE

I will seek daily to be the good father
that God has called me to be.

HOLES AND WOUNDED SOULS

WHEN MY OLDEST SON, JAMIN, was moving out of the toddler years, I started to have a difficult time hugging and kissing him. I wasn't really sure why. But for some reason, it felt strange and well ... just weird. So I decided to talk this situation over with my wife, Yvette. She listened intently as I explained my dilemma. When I finished, without hesitation she said matter-of-factly, "Well, you're just going to have to hold your nose and do it because he needs it ..." So I did. I hugged and hugged and kissed and kissed. And, ironically, I found that the more I did it, the less weird it felt. So much so, that my now thirty-year-old son and his twenty-eight-year old brother Justin still frequently get a "wet one" on the forehead along with a daddy bear hug — or two.

Some years ago, I reflected upon what was going on with me and concluded the following. First, this hugging and kissing thing didn't happen for me because I grew up without my father. I realized that it's difficult to be what you don't see and difficult to give what you didn't have. And, in my case, I didn't see this type of affection from my dad, and so it was hard for me to give it to my own son. In fact, had it not been for my prescient and persuasive wife, I was about to pass on a not-so-good legacy to my sons that I had inherited from my absent father.

Second, I determined that children have a "hole in their soul" in the shape of their dads, and if fathers are unable or unwilling to connect with them physically, emotionally, and spiritually, it can leave a wound that is not easily healed. Admittedly, for much of my life, I was a wounded soul. Truth be told, my difficulty giving the much-needed affection to my son was the result of unhealed wounds from years of feeling neglected and less than worthy. Over the years, I had learned to stuff these feeling away as if they didn't matter, but they clearly did.

Interestingly, it was the act of truly embracing my role as a father that helped to heal me because it required me to love not only my sons, but also myself. It became clear that I couldn't really love my children—the way that God wanted and needed me to—unless I did some "work" on myself.

Finally, I noticed that an interesting thing happened when I hugged and kissed my son. He hugged and kissed me back, even when I didn't expect him to. It was as if he needed to give affection as much as he needed to receive it. And, as a child, so did I, and I guess that I missed something special because I did not have this opportunity with my father.

As I have traveled the country to speak about the importance of fatherhood, I have met other wounded souls—adults and children—who long for the special love and affection that only good fathers can give. Indeed, I am blessed with their burden. It is what motivates me to reach as many fathers as I can as fast as I can, even when the money is short and the days are long. After all, the easiest wound to heal is the one that is never received.[1]

NATIONAL FATHERHOOD INITIATIVE RESOURCES

IN MY MANY YEARS SPEAKING with fathers, especially ones having a challenging time in their role, I would often hear, with longing exasperation, "It's too bad that children don't come with 'how-to' manuals!" I certainly understand the sentiment and desire. However, given the difficulty of labor and delivery, I suspect mothers everywhere are delighted these manuals are not included.

All jokes aside, the fact is there are lots of "how-to" resources available for dads who are committed to developing the skills to be good fathers. In fact, National Fatherhood Initiative (NFI), where I was president for over a decade, is a leading provider of high-quality resources that can help any dad improve his parenting skills, better understand his child's growth and developmental stages, and even improve his relationship with his wife or the mother of his child.

But here's the problem. Too often, I have found that fathers don't seek out and use the excellent resources that are available.

Sadly, many dads spend more time researching and selecting their fantasy football teams than improving their fatherhood skills. These dads treat fantasy football as if it's real and fathering as if it's a fantasy that one can just "pick up" without an investment of time. I am confident that I am on sound theological footing when I say that when you stand before your heavenly Father, he will not ask you about Tom Brady's QB passing rating or Adrian Peterson's average yards per carry. However, he will ask you what you did with the children that were entrusted to you.

So to help prepare you to stand as a good father before your children and before God, I have listed below some selected NFI resources that will help you be the best dad that you can be. But first, to get started, I suggest that you sign up for NFI's free weekly *DadEmail*™ service. It's a fantastic way to get timely and relevant information on a variety of fathering and parenting topics. You can do this easily by going to www.fatherhood.org.

NFI has an impressive selection of brochures and tip cards — in English and Spanish — on a wide range of fatherhood topics such as:

- 10 Ways to Be a Better Dad
- 12 Questions to Ask Before You Become a Father
- So You're a New Dad
- How to Help Your Child Do Well in School
- How to Keep Your Child Healthy
- Helping Your Child Maintain a Healthy Weight

Some helpful guides and interactive resources include:

Help Me Grow: A Dad's Guide to the Ages & Stages of Child Growth. This guide covers everything dads need to know about what to expect and not to expect in terms of child growth over the years. By reviewing the charts in these guides, dads will learn about the physical, mental/emotional, and social changes their children will go through. The guides also include tips for dads to help their children grow.

New Dad's Pocket Guide. With key health and safety information, the *New Dad's Pocket Guide* increases health literacy and equips men with a handy guide they can reference at any time.

Dad's Pocket Guide. It's never been easier to give dads of preschoolers and school-aged children the information they need to stay involved in their children's lives in meaningful ways. An updated version of the popular Dad's Pack, this handy guide has essential hints, tips, and strategies that every dad needs to know.

When Duct Tape Won't Work.™ This is an award-winning, self-paced CD-ROM that gives new dads the information and skills they need to get involved with their children right from the start! With helpful, practical topics and a fun, engaging format, *When Duct Tape Won't Work* builds new fathers' health literacy as they learn important child health and safety information and skills. Accessible and engaging, *When Duct Tape Won't Work* increases confidence and knowledge so that dads can successfully care for their newborn/toddler.

Deployed Fathers and Family Guide. Used by all branches of the armed forces, this practical guide is filled with helpful tips, exercises, and strategies to help military fathers and their families prepare for and successfully navigate deployment challenges.

NFI is also the leading provider of fatherhood curricula for individual and group study. Here are a few that might be helpful for you:

24/7 Dad® Power Hour. Developed by seasoned ministers, *24/7 Dad Power Hour* is a revolutionary and innovative individual or small group study that helps men, through podcasts, videos, and one-hour gatherings, explore God's intentions and design for fathers and families. A father will be encouraged to "Reach Up" to God and "Reach Out" to his wife (or the mother of the children) and children with activities and solid strategies to strengthen his relationships at home. There are three engaging studies with six one-hour sessions each:

1. The Christian Dad: Your Calling, Privileges, and Responsibilities
2. Fatherhood and the Christian Dad
3. Relationships and the Christian Dad

If you are seeking to reach dads in your church or community, the below resources may be of interest to you.

Men's Ministry Remodeled™ (Downloadable "eProduct"). Involved fathers are strong leaders for their families and for your congregation or community. Strengthen the fathers and families in your community with this comprehensive guide. *Men's Ministry Remodeled* is a one-year plan that churches and ministries can use to establish a sustainable men's ministry that prioritizes fathers. This program provides the tools needed to create an intentional men's ministry where fathers feel welcomed and encouraged.

Doctor Dad.[*] Reach new and expectant dads when they need it most with child health and safety workshops. Doctor Dad helps increase fathers' health literacy by providing men with the knowledge and skills they need to successfully care for their young children right from the start.

InsideOut Dad.[*] Now in its second edition, *InsideOut Dad* is the nation's only evidence-based fatherhood program designed specifically for incarcerated fathers. Standardized programming for twenty-four states and New York City, *InsideOut Dad* helps reduce recidivism rates by reconnecting incarcerated fathers to their families, providing the motivation to get out and stay out. The program features both a secular version and a Christian version, which was developed in partnership with Prison Fellowship. It's a great curriculum for a church-based prison ministry outreach.

The 7 Habits of a 24/7 Dad. This resource is an eight-hour workshop that combines the fundamental fathering principles from National Fatherhood Initiative's 24/7 Dad programs with the late Dr. Stephen Covey's timeless seven habits, making it easier than ever to engage fathers! This activity-filled workshop guides men as they adopt and apply seven helpful habits that will revolutionize their fathering skills and help them connect with their kids.

DadVentures and DadVentures-Preschool. Filled with fun activities that kids and dads can do together, this interactive curriculum teaches children important character traits and connects kids directly with their dads for a fun time they'll never forget. Fathers will learn how to communicate important values and character traits to their children as they grow and play together. Dads will learn how to relate to their kids as they participate in fun activities like learning how to use a compass and whistling with a blade of grass.

These great fatherhood resources, along with others that you will find at www.fatherhood.org, in bookstores, and on the web, will help you avoid the "bad dad mistakes" and be the father that God wants you to be and that your kids need you to be. So be encouraged and be diligent. And, as 2 Timothy 2:15 reminds us, do your best to present yourself to God — as a father — as one approved, a worker who does not need to be ashamed.

NOTES

CHAPTER 1: A CLARION CALL TO FATHERS

1. The Barna Group, "The Spirituality of Moms Outpaces That of Dads," May 7, 2007. *http://www.barna.org/family-kids-articles/104-the-spirituality-of-moms-outpaces-that-of-dads?q=2007.*
2. Robbie Low, "The Truth about Men and Church," June 2003. *http://www.touchstonemag.com/archives/article.php?id=16–05–024-v*
3. National Fatherhood Initiative, *Father Facts*, 6th ed. (Germantown, Md.: National Fatherhood Initiative, 2011), 23.
4. National Fatherhood Initiative, *Pop's Culture: A National Survey of Dads' Attitudes on Fathering* (Germantown, Md.: National Fatherhood Initiative, 2006), 2–3.
5. National Fatherhood Initiative, *Mama Says: A National Survey of Mothers' Attitudes on Fathering* (Germantown, Md.: National Fatherhood Initiative, 2009), 27.

CHAPTER 3: LABAN: HE MADE HIS CHILDREN COMPETE FOR HIS AFFECTION

1. John Mayer, *VH1 Storytellers*, August 27, 2010. *http://www.vh1.com/video/misc/556092/daughters-live-from-vh1-storytellers.jhtml*
2. Jonetta Rose Barras, *Whatever Happened to Daddy's Little Girl?* (New York: Random House, 2000), 1.

CHAPTER 4: JACOB: HE TURNED A BLIND EYE TO SIBLING RIVALRY

1. Katy Butler, "Beyond Rivalry, a Hidden World of Sibling Violence," *The New York Times*, February 28, 2006. *http://www.nytimes.com/2006/02/28/health/28sibl.html?pagewanted=all*

2. Ari Odzer, "Brother vs. Brother: Self-Defense?" *NBC News Miami*, October 29, 2009. *http://www.nbcmiami.com/news/local/brother-vs-brother-self-defense-67288532.html*

3. Associated Press, "Florida Teen Allegedly Kills Younger Brother Over Loud Music," *FoxNews*, October 28, 2009. *http://www.foxnews.com/story/0,2933,570145,00.html*

4. Kyla Boyse and Brenda Volling, "Sibling Rivalry," University of Michigan Health System, October 2011. *www.med.umich.edu/yourchild/topics/sibriv.htm*

CHAPTER 5: SAUL: HE MADE IT DIFFICULT FOR HIS CHILDREN TO HONOR HIM

1. David Voreacos and David Glovin, "Madoff Confessed to $50 Billion Fraud before FBI Arrest," *Bloomberg*, December 12, 2008. *http://www.bloomberg.com/apps/news?pid=newsarchive&sid=atUk.QnXAvZY*

2. James Bandler and Nicholas Varchaver, "How Bernie Did It," *CNN Money*, April 30, 2009. *http://money.cnn.com/2009/04/24/news/newsmakers/madoff.fortune.index.htm*

3. Ibid.

4. Ibid.

5. Ibid.

6. Ibid.

7. Robert Frank, Amir Efrati, Arron Lucchetti, and Chad Bray, "Madoff Jailed after Admitting Epic Scam," *Wall Street Journal*, May 13, 2009. *http://online.wsj.com/article/SB123685693449906551.html?mod=djemalertNEWS*

8. Ibid.

9. Binyamin Appelbaum, David S. Hilzenrath, and Amit R. Paley, "All Just One Big Lie," *Washington Post*, December 13, 2008.

10. C. Brand, C. Draper, A. England, S. Bond, E. R. Clendenen, T. C. Bulter, and B. Latta, *Holman Illustrated Bible Dictionary* (Nashville: Holman, 2003), 1473–74.

11. "Ruth and Andrew Madoff," *60 Minutes*, October 30, 2011. *http://www.cbsnews.com/video/watch/?id=7386490n*

12. Ibid.

CHAPTER 6: ABRAHAM: HE ABANDONED HIS CHILD

1. Andrea F. Siegel and Kimberly A. C. Wilson, "Malvo Depicted as Sad, Sinister," *Baltimore Sun*, November 14, 2003. *http://www.baltimoresun. com/news/maryland/bal-te.md.malvo14nov14,0,3703556.story?page=1*

2. Andrea F. Siegel and Julie Scharper, "DC Sniper Tells Jury of Lethal Bomb Plots," *Los Angeles Times*, May 24, 2006. *http://articles.latimes. com/2006/may/24/nation/na-sniper24*

3. Josh White, "Notorious Young Sniper Lee Malvo: 'I was a monster,'" *Seattle Times*, updated September 30, 2012. *http://seattletimes.com/ html/nationworld/2019300881_snipermalvo30.html*

4. Ian Sager and Scott Stump, "DC Sniper Lee Boyd Malvo: 'I was sexually abused by my accomplice,'" *Today News,* October 24, 2012. *http://todaynews.today.com/_news/2012/10/24/14680073-dc-sniper-lee-boyd-malvo-i-was-sexually-abused-by-my-accomplice?lite*

5. Matthew Hay Brown, "Accused Boy's Fate a Tale of 2 Fathers," *Hartford Courant*, October 27, 2002. *http://articles.courant. com/2002 – 10 – 27/news/0210270763_1_leslie-malvo-lee-boyd-malvo-burned-out-traffic-lights*

6. Robert Mendick, "Norway Massacre: The Real Anders Behring Brievik," *The Telegraph,* July 31, 2011. *http://articles.courant. com/2002 – 10 – 27/news/02010270763 – 1 – leslie – malvo-lee – boyd-malvo-burned-out-traffic-lights*

7. Jon Henley, "Anders Behring Breivik Trial: The Father's Story," *The Guardian*, April 13, 2012. *http://www.guardian.co.uk/world/2012/ apr/13/anders-behring-breivik-norway*

8. "Norway Killer: Anders Behring Breivik was a mummy's boy," *The Telegraph*, July 25, 2011. *http://www.telegraph.co.uk/news/worldnews/ europe/norway/8659746/Norway-killer-Anders-Behring-Breivik-was-a-mummys-boy.html*

9. "Anders Behring Breivik's Father: 'My son should have taken his own life,'" *The Telegraph*, July 25, 2011. *http://www.telegraph.co.uk/news/ worldnews/europe/norway/8660397/Anders-Behring-Breiviks-father-My-son-should-have-taken-his-own-life.html*

10. "Eminem's Incredible Rise to Stardom," *60 Minutes*, October 10, 2010, updated August 2, 2011. *http://www.cbsnews. com/8301 – 18560_162 – 20086920.html?pageNum=3*

11. National Fatherhood Initiative, *Father Facts*, 6th ed. (Germantown, Md.: National Fatherhood Initiative, 2011), 18.

12. William S. Aquilino, "The Noncustodial Father-Child Relationship from Adolescence into Young Adulthood," *Journal of Marriage and Family* 68, no. 4 (November 2006): 929–46.
13. National Fatherhood Initiative, *Father Facts*, 6th ed. (Germantown, Md.: National Fatherhood Initiative, 2011), 66–77.
14. S. Truett Cathy, *It's Better to Build Boys Than Mend Men* (Decatur, Ga.: Looking Glass Books, 2004), 10.

CHAPTER 7: ELI: HE FAILED TO DISCIPLINE HIS CHILDREN

1. The Inquisitr, "Stating the obvious, Amy Winehouse fears early death" (December 28, 2008). *http://www.inquisitr.com/13488/stating-the-obvious-amy-winehouse-fears-early-death/*
2. Mitch Winehouse, *Amy, My Daughter* (New York: HarperCollins, 2012), 53.
3. Ibid.
4. Ibid., 54.
5. Ibid.
6. Ibid., 4.
7. Ibid., 8.
8. Ibid., 19.
9. Mitch Winehouse, *Rush of Love*, "Mitch's Biography." *http://www.mitchwinehouse.co.uk/about/*
10. Josh McDowell, "Rules without Relationships Leads to Rebellion," Power to Change. *http://powertochange.com/experience/spiritual-growth/relationships-that-transform–9/*

CHAPTER 8: MANOAH: HE FAILED TO TAME HIS CHILD'S TALENTS

1. M. Easton, *Easton's Bible Dictionary* (Oak Harbor, Wash.: Logos Research Systems, Inc., 1996).
2. Walter A. Elwell, *Baker Commentary on the Bible* (Grand Rapids: Baker, 1989), 172.

CHAPTER 9: LOT: HE PITCHED HIS FAMILY'S TENT NEAR TEMPTATION

1. Joyce Ostin, *Hollywood Dads* (San Francisco: Chronicle Books, 2007).

2. Pamela Paul, "From Pornography to Porno to Porn: How Porn Became the Norm," in *The Social Costs of Pornography: A Collection of Papers* (Princeton, N.J.: Witherspoon Institute, Inc., 2010).

3. Ibid.

4. Philip G. Zimbardo and Nikita Duncan, "The Demise of Guys: How Video Games and Porn Are Ruining a Generation," *CNN Health*, May 24, 2012. *http://www.cnn.com/2012/05/23/health/living-well/demise-of-guys/index.html*

5. Bill Perkins, *When Good Men Are Tempted* (Grand Rapids: Zondervan, 1997), 123.

6. Ibid., 129.

CHAPTER 10: 6 THINGS A DAD MUST DO TO BE A GOOD FATHER

1. William Evans, *The Great Doctrines of the Bible* (Chicago: Moody Press, 1974), 319.

2. Sager and Stump, "DC Sniper Lee Boyd Malvo" (see chap. 6, n. 4).

3. National Fatherhood Initiative, *Pop's Culture: A National Survey of Dads' Attitudes on Fathering* (Germantown, Md.: National Fatherhood Initiative, 2006), 16.

4. Stephen R. Covey, *The 8th Habit: From Effectiveness to Greatness* (New York: Free Press, 2004), 165.

5. Roland C. Warren, "Are You Robbing Your Kids?" *The Father Factor*, National Fatherhood Initiative, April 21, 2011. *http://blog.fatherhood.org/bid/135524/Are-You-Trying-to-Rob-Your-Kids*. Used with permission.

6. Allen G. Breed and Binaj Gurubacharya, "Everest Remains Deadly Draw for Climbers," *USA Today*, July 16, 2006. *http://usatoday30.usatoday.com/tech/science/2006–07–16-everest-david-sharp_x.htm*

7. Ibid.

8. Christian A. Scheller, "Q & A: John Piper on Racism, Reconciliation, and Theology after Trayvon Martin's Death," *Christianity Today*, March 30, 2012. *http://www.christianitytoday.com/ct/2012/marchweb-only/john-piper-racism-reconciliation.html?start=3*

9. Ibid.

10. "12 Ways to Love a Wayward Child," *Desiring God*, May 9, 2007.

http://www.desiringgod.org/resource-library/taste-see-articles/12-ways-to-love-your-wayward-child

11. "Become a Double Duty Dad," *National Fatherhood Initiative. http://www.fatherhood.org/get-involved/double-duty-dad*

12. "Closing the Mentoring Gap," *Mentor. http://www.mentoring.org/about_mentor/value_of_mentoring/closing_the_mentoring_gap/*

13. J. B. Grossman and J. E. Rhodes, "The Test of Time: Predictors and Effects of Duration in Youth Mentoring Programs," *American Journal of Community Psychology* 30 (2002): 196–206.

APPENDIX A: HOLES AND WOUNDED SOULS

1. Roland Warren, "Dads Healing Holes and Wounded Souls," *Sojourners*, June 15, 2009. *http://sojo.net/blogs/2009/06/15/dads-healing-holes-and-wounded-souls.* Used with permission.

ABOUT THE AUTHOR

ROLAND WARREN was born in Toledo, Ohio, and received his undergraduate degree from Princeton University and an MBA from the University of Pennsylvania's Wharton School of Business. After nearly twenty years working in the business world for IBM, PepsiCo, and Goldman Sachs & Co., he spent over a decade as president of National Fatherhood Initiative, whose mission is to improve the well-being of children by increasing the proportion of children growing up with involved, responsible, and committed fathers. NFI is now the leading provider of fatherhood resources to help fathers improve their skills and relationships.

Roland is currently president and CEO of Care Net, whose 1,180 centers make it one of the largest network of pregnancy care centers, with affiliates in the US and Canada. Care Net's Christ-centered mission is to promote a culture of life within our society in order to serve women and men facing unplanned pregnancies.

Roland is a much sought after keynote speaker on topics ranging from fatherhood to marriage and the family in the national media. He has appeared on *The Oprah Winfrey Show*, *Oprah's Life Classes*, *The Today Show*, *Fox and Friends*, CNN, C-SPAN, Fox News Channel, and Black Entertainment Television. He has been interviewed by major radio and newspaper outlets such as *The New York Times*, *The Wall Street Journal*, *USA Today*, *The Washington Post*, *O* magazine, *Ebony*, *Sports Illustrated*, *Christianity Today*, *Essence*, the *Tavis Smiley Show*, *Life Style*, *Janet Parshall's*

America, Focus on the Family, and *Disney Radio.* He also has written a monthly column called "Pop Culture" for *The Washington Times* and has had articles published in *CNN, The Washington Post, The Huffington Post, Washington Post's* The Root, and *Christianity Today.*

Roland stays active in church, community, and civic activities. He served on the Fatherhood Task Force of the White House Office of Faith-Based and Neighborhood Partnerships and on the Coordinating Council on Juvenile Justice and Delinquency Prevention for the US Department of Justice. He is currently on the board of World Vision, National Fatherhood Initiative, and Christian Union. A resident of Middletown, Maryland, Roland has been married to Dr. Yvette Lopez-Warren for over thirty years and has two adult sons, Jamin and Justin.

Share Your Thoughts

With the Author: Your comments will be forwarded to the author when you send them to *zauthor@zondervan.com*.

With Zondervan: Submit your review of this book by writing to *zreview@zondervan.com*.

Free Online Resources at
www.zondervan.com

Daily Bible Verses and Devotions: Enrich your life with daily Bible verses or devotions that help you start every morning focused on God. Visit www.zondervan.com/newsletters.

Free Email Publications: Sign up for newsletters on Christian living, academic resources, church ministry, fiction, children's resources, and more. Visit www.zondervan.com/newsletters.

Zondervan Bible Search: Find and compare Bible passages in a variety of translations at www.zondervanbiblesearch.com.

Other Benefits: Register to receive online benefits like coupons and special offers, or to participate in research.